Best E

Best Easy Day Hikes Palm Springs and Coachella Valley

Second Edition

Bruce Grubbs

FALCONGUIDES

GUILFORD, CONNECTICUT
HELENA, MONTANA

FALCONGUIDES®

An imprint of The Rowman & Littlefield Publishing Group, Inc.
4501 Forbes Blvd., Ste. 200
Lanham, MD 20706
www.rowman.com

Falcon and FalconGuides are registered trademarks and Make Adventure Your Story is a trademark of The Rowman & Littlefield Publishing Group, Inc.

Distributed by NATIONAL BOOK NETWORK

British Library Cataloguing-in-Publication Information available

Library of Congress Cataloging-in-Publication Data available

ISBN 978-1-4930-4113-8 (paperback)
ISBN 978-1-4930-4114-5 (e-book)

♾™ The paper used in this publication meets the minimum requirements of American National Standard for Information Sciences—Permanence of Paper for Printed Library Materials, ANSI/NISO Z39.48-1992.

Printed in the United States of America

Contents

The Hikes

Palm Springs

Indian Canyons

Palms to Pines

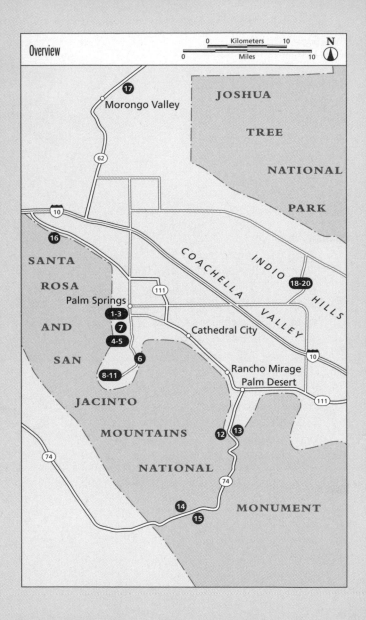

Acknowledgments

Special thanks to Jim Foote, Santa Rosa and San Jacinto Mountains National Monument, and Therese Everett-Kerley, Indian Canyons, for reviewing the manuscript. I would also like to thank my many hiking companions down the years, who've put up with my incessant trail mapping and photography. Thanks to Duart Martin, for her constant support and encouragement. And thanks to my editors and Rowman & Littlefield, David Legere and Alex Bordelon, for turning my rough manuscript into a polished book. Finally, thanks to Melissa Baker for her usual fine work on the maps.

Introduction

When most people think of Palm Springs, they think of Hollywood celebrities and major golf tournaments. The residents of Palm Springs who are hikers know better. They know that the desert city is bordered on the immediate west and south by Santa Rosa and San Jacinto Mountains National Monument, as well as the Agua Caliente Indian Reservation, which contains the Indian Canyons. Hikes in these areas are just a few minutes from Palm Springs. There are also some great trails just a little farther from Palm Springs along the Palms to Pines Highway (CA 74). Big Morongo Canyon Preserve, about an hour north of Palm Springs, features a small loop trail system through the preserve's wetlands, as well as a scenic trail along Big Morongo Canyon itself. Coachella Valley Preserve, just east of Palm Springs, has an extensive network of hiking trails.

Towering above the city and snowcapped in winter, the high country of the San Jacinto and Santa Rosa Mountains are a summer hiker's paradise, but are beyond the scope of this guide.

Much of the two mountain ranges that border Palm Springs on the west and south are contained in the Santa Rosa and San Jacinto Mountains National Monument, which is jointly managed by the Bureau of Land Management and the U.S. Forest Service.

The Indian Canyons, which include Tahquitz Canyon and lower Palm Canyon and its tributaries, are owned and managed by the Agua Caliente Band of Cahuilla Indians.

The Palms to Pines Highway connects Palm Desert and adjoining cities to Idyllwild and the high country of the San

Jacinto Mountains. Several of the hikes in this book are at intermediate elevations along the highway.

Big Morongo Canyon Preserve lies at the east end of the Little San Bernardino Mountains, and preserves a large wetlands as well as Big Morongo Canyon.

Coachella Valley Preserve is just east of Palm Springs. The preserve protects rolling desert hills and several palm oasis sites, as well as interesting geology.

Geology

The Santa Rosa and San Jacinto Mountains represent the northern end of the Peninsular Ranges, which form the mountainous spine of Baja California and extend north into the Palm Springs region. The San Andreas Fault zone runs though the adjoining Coachella Valley, and is the area where the Pacific and North American continental plates are colliding. As the two continental plates move past each other, something has to give—and that something is the rocks as they shatter along fault lines. The basic movement along the faults is horizontal, but these immense forces also cause mountain ranges to rise and valley floors to drop. Although the San Andreas Fault itself is the most famous, there are many other active faults in this fault zone.

Because of this active geology, the topography in the vicinity of Palm Springs is dramatic. The mountains surrounding Palm Springs are fault block ranges that have been raised to their present lofty altitudes by vertical movement along the numerous faults that bisect the area. The mass of rock that makes up these mountains is part of the Southern California Batholith, a body of light-colored granite and related rocks that formed as magma slowly solidified into solid rock deep underground. Metamorphic rocks such as schist are found on the eastern slopes of the San Jacintos. Under intense heat and pressure, these rocks were transformed from their sedimentary origins into new forms without ever actually melting.

Plants and Animals

The life zone concept is used to explain how plant communities tend to group at different altitudes. Because the mountains become wetter and cooler as you ascend, different plant communities and the animals that depend on them tend to thrive at different altitudes. At the base of the mountains, in the Coachella Valley, you are in the Colorado Desert, the western division of the Sonoran Desert—one of the four major North American deserts. This area lies at or below sea level. As you ascend the east slopes of Mount San Jacinto, you'll pass through four more life zones, culminating in the arctic-alpine life zone around the summit. Because of this great range in elevation—one of the largest in the United States—there is a corresponding diversity of plants and animals.

Runoff from snowmelt and summer storms creates many permanent streams in the canyons flanking the high mountains. Other water comes to the surface in the form of springs, where groundwater is dammed along faults and forced to the surface. In the desert foothills, many of these springs support oases of California fan palms, which other plants, as well as birds and animals, use as green, cool, and sheltered refuges from the surrounding desert.

After a wet winter and spring, if conditions are just right, the desert comes alive with an unbelievable display of wildflowers. Although it's difficult to predict the flower display in a given year, it's worth making the effort to hike in a good flower year. Some flowers, such as Indian paintbrush, start to bloom as early as February, but the main display is reserved for March and April. Cactus such as barrel, prickly pear, and hedgehog tend to bloom in April and May. Check www .desertusa.com for flower updates throughout the desert.

Weather

Climate varies with elevation and aspect, as the higher mountains and west-facing slopes wring more moisture out of passing storms. The lofty mountains tend to intercept much of the moisture from storms moving west off the Pacific Ocean, creating a rain shadow on their eastern sides. Palm Springs gets less than 6 inches of precipitation per year, and nearly every day is sunny. It's common for Palm Springs residents to look up and see snowstorms swirling around the 10,000-foot summits to the west while the city on the desert floor is basking in warm sunshine.

Most of the hikes in this book lie at low elevations, where the summer heat is intense, often producing daily highs above 110 degrees F. Temperatures drop rapidly at night due to the dry, clear air, so nights can be chilly. It is best to hike early in the morning during the summer. During late summer, there are occasional outbreaks of afternoon thunderstorm activity. During these periods, hike early, and get off exposed ridges and summits before thunderstorms form and lightning begins to strike.

Fall and spring are very pleasant in the foothills, as temperatures max out in the 80s. Nights can be chilly, as the temperature often drops forty or fifty degrees from the afternoon high. Fall brings dry, stable weather, even on the high summits, while spring can bring stunning displays of wildflowers if winter and spring rains have been plentiful.

Winter in Palm Springs sees temperatures topping out in the 70s, and it's always a little cooler just above the city in the Santa Rosa and San Jacinto foothills. Although nighttime temperatures can drop below freezing, the dry, stable weather means that even winter is a good hiking season.

The best source for up-to-date weather information is the National Weather Service in San Diego; the website is www.weather.gov/sandiego. Commercial weather sources concentrate on urban areas and highway corridors, but by using the National Weather Service website, you can click on a map and get a specific point forecast for the trail you plan to hike. This is important because the weather in the mountains is usually much different than the weather in the city.

Hazards and Environmental Considerations

- In the desert, even in the winter when the air is cool, dehydration is a serious concern. Because the humidity is usually very low, your body loses moisture insensibly. Carry and drink plenty of water, and eat high energy snacks for fuel and to help keep your electrolytes in balance. As the temperature rises in the spring, these measures are even more necessary to prevent heat exhaustion, which can develop into life-threatening sunstroke.

- Don't cut switchbacks. It takes more effort and increases erosion.

- You will encounter mountain bikers outside designated wilderness areas. Although technically hikers have the right of way, because bicycles are less maneuverable, it's polite to step aside so the riders can pass without having to veer off the trail.

- Smokers should stop at a bare spot or rock ledge, then make certain that all smoking materials are out before continuing. Due to fire hazard, it may be illegal to smoke while traveling in the backcountry. Never smoke or light any kind of fire on windy days or when the fire danger is high, because wildfires can start easily and spread explosively.

- Although dogs are allowed in some of the areas covered by this book, it is your responsibility to keep them from barking and bothering wildlife or other hikers, and to pick up after them. Some of the hikes are in critical habitat for the endangered peninsular bighorn sheep, where dogs are strictly prohibited because their mere presence is enough to cause the bighorn to leave the area.

- Don't cut live trees or plants of any kind, carve on trees or rocks, pick wildflowers, or build structures such as rock campfire rings.

- Motorized vehicles are prohibited on all the trails in this book.

- Some trails are open to horses. When encountering horses, step off the trail, stand quietly, and talk to the riders in a normal tone.

- If you carried it in, you can also carry it out. Do not bury food or trash. Animals will dig it up. They become dependent on human food, which can lead to unpleasant encounters and cause the animal to starve during the off-season.

- A short walk in any popular recreation area will show you that few people seem to know how to answer the call of nature away from facilities. Diseases such as giardiasis are spread by poor human sanitation. If facilities are available, use them. In the backcountry, select a site at least 100 yards from streams, lakes, springs, and dry washes. Avoid barren, sandy soil, if possible. Next, dig a small "cat-hole" about 6 inches down into the organic layer of the soil. (Some people carry a small plastic trowel for this purpose.) When finished, refill the hole, and carry out used toilet paper in doubled zipper plastic bags.

- The desert foothills around Palm Springs have several varieties of cactus, notably several species of cholla. Most species of cholla cactus propagate by means of joints, outer segments of branches that easily break off and cling to animals or humans that brush against them. Cholla cactus spines are fine, sharp, and microscopically barbed. You'll need a comb or a pair of sticks to dislodge the joints. Deeply embedded cholla spines, often a result of falling on a cactus, may require a visit to a doctor. Dogs are especially adept at getting cholla spines deeply embedded in their mouths, which may require a visit to the vet.

- Plenty of other desert plants have developed spines for defense. Some agaves and yuccas have stiff swordlike leaves with sharp points that can do serious damage to the desert explorer unlucky enough to fall on one. Catclaw is a low bush that often grows in thickets and is covered with curved spines that catch on clothing and skin. All these sharp bits of plant tend to end up on the ground, so check the ground carefully before you sit down or set up a tent.

- Animals will normally leave you alone unless molested or provoked. Do not ever feed wild animals, as they rapidly get used to the handouts and then will vigorously defend their new food source. Bears in particular will defend a food source.

- Although it is extremely rare, mountain lions have been known to attack people. If you encounter a mountain lion or a bear, move away slowly and give the animal space to retreat. At close quarters, do not turn your back on a mountain lion, and do not run. Pick up small children, make eye contact with the lion, and make yourself as large as possible. Lions normally attack deer from ambush and avoid direct fights. If attacked, fight back with anything at hand.

- Rattlesnakes cause concern among inexperienced hikers but can easily be avoided. They usually warn off intruders by rattling well before you reach striking range. Since rattlesnakes can strike no farther than half their body length, avoid placing your hands and feet in areas you cannot see, and walk several feet away from rock overhangs and shady ledges. Snakes prefer surfaces at about 80 degrees, so during hot weather they prefer the shade of bushes or rock overhangs, and in cool weather will be found sunning themselves on open ground.

Zero Impact

Three Falcon Zero-Impact Principles:

- Leave with everything you brought.
- Leave no sign of your visit.
- Leave the landscape as you found it.

Gear Every Hiker Should Carry:

- Water
- Food
- Sun hat
- Sunscreen
- Sunglasses
- Durable hiking shoes or boots
- Synthetic fleece jacket or pullover
- Rain gear
- Map
- Compass
- First-aid kit
- Signal mirror
- Toilet paper and zippered plastic bags

How to Use This Guide

This book is broken into five sections, covering hikes in the San Jacinto and Santa Rosa foothills on the west and south edges of Palm Springs, the Indian Canyons adjacent to Palm Springs, hikes reached from the Palms to Pines Highway, hikes north of Palm Springs, and hikes in the Coachella Valley Preserve east of Palm Springs. All of the hikes are less than one hour's drive from Palm Springs, and many are just a few minutes away.

Using the Trail Descriptions

Each hike in the book has a number and name. Some trails have more than one common name, and other hikes use more than one trail to complete a loop or otherwise create a more interesting route. In each case, I've attempted to name the hike for the best-known trail or feature. Each hike starts with a general description of the highlights and attractions. A summary of the hike follows, with at-a-glance information.

- Distance: This is the total mileage of the hike. For out-and-back hikes, it includes the return mileage. Loop hikes include the total distance around the loop. Some loops may have an out-and-back section, or cherry stem. I've selected hikes that do not require a car shuttle, for simplicity and so that you can spend more of your hiking time on the trail instead of in a car. Distances were measured on digital topographic maps and may vary slightly from official mileages, but are consistent throughout the book.

- Approximate hiking time: This is based on an average hiker who is reasonably fit. More casual hikers should allow more time. The hiking time does not include time for lunch stops, wildlife viewing, photography, or other distractions. Plan on more time for such activities. Groups should remember that the party travels at the speed of the slowest member.

- Difficulty: All hikes in this book are rated easy or moderate. There are no strenuous or difficult hikes, but sections of trails may be steep, rough, or otherwise more strenuous than the overall rating would indicate. Just about anyone should be able to do an easy hike. Moderate hikes require a bit of fitness, and beginners should allow extra time.

- Trail surface: This describes the type of tread you'll be walking on.

- Best season: Most of the hikes are at low desert elevations, and the best season for these is October through March. If you do these hikes during the summer, get a very early start, take plenty of water, and plan to be done by midmorning, before the day's heat sets in. Two of the hikes, Upper Palm Canyon and Cactus Spring Trail, are at intermediate elevations and can be hiked all year, though it will still be hot in midsummer.

- Water availability: Although day hikers should carry all the water they need, this section lists known water sources for emergency use. All water should be purified before drinking.

- Other trail users: These may include equestrians and mountain bikers.

- Canine compatibility: If dogs are allowed, they must be on a leash. This is just common courtesy to other hikers, some of whom may have had bad experiences with dogs. If your dog barks or runs up to other hikers, even in a friendly way, you are giving dog owners a bad name. Always clean up after your dog.

- Maps: Each hike has a map showing the trail and any pertinent landmarks. Hikers wishing to explore farther should carry the U.S. Geological Survey topographic maps listed in this section. These are the most detailed maps for terrain and natural features, but do not show all trails.

- Fees and permits: Tahquitz Canyon and the Indian Canyons charge an entrance fee. Permits are not required for any of the hikes in this book.

- Trail contact: This section lists the name, address, phone, and Web site of the managing agency or best contact for trail information. It's a good idea to contact the agency for up-to-date trail information before your hike.

- Special considerations: This section covers trail hazards and environmental hazards during certain times of the year.

- Finding the trailhead: Trailhead directions are from the junction of South Palm Canyon Drive and East Palm Canyon Drive in Palm Springs. GPS coordinates for each trailhead are given in latitude/longitude format using the WGS84 datum. If you prefer UTM, you can convert with sites such as https://www.geoplaner.com.

- The hike: This is a narrative description of the hike route and attractions you'll find along the way. There are also descriptions of relevant natural or human history.

- Miles and directions: This lists the key points, such as trail intersections, by miles and tenths. You should be able to follow the route with this information alone.

The mileages in this book do not necessarily agree with distances found on trail signs, agency mileages, and other descriptions, because trail miles are measured by a variety of methods and personnel. All mileages in this book were carefully measured using digital topographic mapping software for accuracy and consistency.

Share the Trail

Some of the trails in this book are open to horseback riders and/or mountain bikers as well as hikers. Horses always have the right of way over hikers and cyclists, both of which should move off the trail downhill and remain still until the horses have passed. Talking quietly to the riders helps convince the horses that you are a person and not some weird monster with a hump on its back. Don't make sudden movements or noises.

Technically, hikers have the right of way over cyclists, but in practice it's more reasonable for hikers to step off the trail to avoid forcing the riders off trail. On their part, cyclists should be courteous, always ride under control, and warn hikers of their approach.

Trail Finder

Best Hikes for Geology Lovers

Best Hikes for Children

Best Hikes for Dogs

Best Hikes for Great Views

Legend

═══⟨10⟩═══	Interstate Highway
───⟨74⟩───	State Highway
═══════	County or Local Road
───────	River or Creek
─··─··─··	Intermittent Stream
▬▬▬▬▬▬	Featured Trail
- - - - - -	Trail
‿̑	Bridge
⚠	Campground
🅿	Parking
‿	Pass
▲	Peak
🛆	Picnic Area
▪	Point of Interest
🚻	Restrooms
⌐	Spring
❶	Trailhead
🖼	Viewpoint
❓	Visitor Center
≋	Waterfall

Palm Springs

These trails start right on the edge of Palm Springs, in the foothills of the San Jacinto and northern Santa Rosa Mountains. Since they are only a few minutes' drive from most of the city, they are very convenient, whether you're a resident or a visitor staying in Palm Springs.

1 North Carl Lykken Trail to Falls Overlook

The north end of the Carl Lykken Trail system doesn't get as much use as the other trailheads, and it's just as scenic. A steep but short climb leads to a saddle and viewpoint, followed by a scenic traverse along the base of the San Jacinto Mountains. Finally, you climb to a point on a ridge overlooking a seasonal waterfall.

Distance: 4.6 miles out and back
Approximate hiking time: 2 hours
Difficulty: Moderate
Trail surface: Dirt and rocks
Best season: Oct through Mar
Water availability: None
Other trail users: Mountain bikes and horses
Canine compatibility: Dogs not allowed
Maps: USGS Palm Springs; Santa Rosa and San Jacinto Mountains National Monument Trail Map

Fees and permits: None
Trail contact: Santa Rosa and San Jacinto Mountains National Monument Visitor Center, 51-500 Highway 74, Palm Desert, CA 92260; (760) 862-9984; www.blm.gov/ca/st/en/fo/palm springs/santarosa.html
Special considerations: During the summer hike early in the day, carry plenty of water, and plan to be finished with the hike by midmorning.

Finding the trailhead: From Palm Springs at the intersection of East Palm Canyon Drive and South Palm Canyon Drive, drive north on South Palm Canyon Drive until it crosses Tahquitz Canyon Way. After 3 miles, turn left on Vista Chino Drive. Continue 0.3 mile and then turn right on Via Norte. Drive 0.1 mile and then turn left on West Chino

Canyon Drive. After 0.2 mile, turn left on Panorama Drive and continue 0.5 mile to the unsigned trailhead in a small cul-de-sac on the left, just before the end of the road. GPS: N33° 50.722' W116° 33.694'

The Hike

The North Carl Lykken Trail climbs the steep slope south of the trailhead in a series of short and very steep switchbacks. The upside of the steep climb is that the trail quickly reaches a saddle with a good view of the north end of Palm Springs. You can also see the trail ahead, cutting across the lower slopes of the mountains. A gentle descent via a couple of broad switchbacks leads to a point where the trail levels out just above the base of the mountainside.

After contouring south along this slope, the North Carl Lykken Trail crosses the bajada slope at the mouth of a short, steep, unnamed canyon. A bajada slope forms along the base of a desert mountain range where outwash debris fans from several adjacent canyons merge to form a broad, gentle slope of flood debris. The bajada lies between the base of the steep mountain slopes and the flat valley floor. This bajada slope is quite small, mainly consisting of the debris from the nameless canyon and Tachevah Canyon farther along the trail. Some bajada slopes run for miles along the base of the mountains, and may even meet the bajada slope from an adjacent mountain range, forming a valley with a shallow V-shaped profile.

From the bajada, the trail descends slightly, then follows the base of the mountainside and emerges into the outwash plain of Tachevah Canyon. At a junction, stay left on the North Carl Lykken Trail. The trail climbs steeply up a north-facing slope to a viewpoint on the ridge crest overlooking a seasonal waterfall. In the spring after a wet winter, snowmelt can send a good flow over the fall. At other times it may be

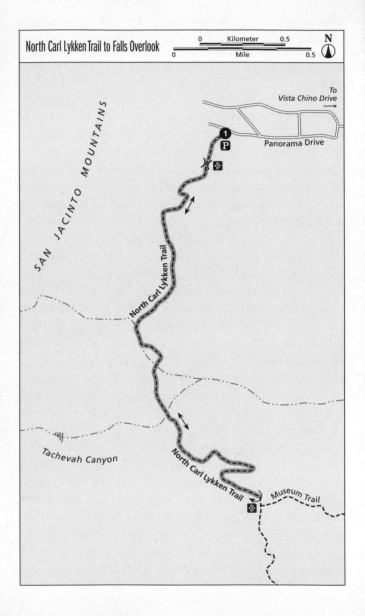

a trickle. The granite cliffs in this area are also popular with rock climbers, and you may see or hear them on the cliffs.

Miles and Directions

0.0 Start at the trailhead.

0.2 Reach the saddle and viewpoint.

0.7 The trail levels out and contours south near the base of the slope.

1.0 Cross a broad bajada slope.

1.3 Skirt the base of the mountain slope.

1.5 At the trail junction, stay left on the North Carl Lykken Trail and follow it south to the top of the ridge.

2.3 Arrive at viewpoint. Return the way you came.

4.6 Arrive back at the trailhead.

2 North Carl Lykken Trail to Museum Trail

The south end of the North Carl Lykken Trail climbs steadily up the steep mountain slopes above Palm Springs, winding through granite boulders to a point on a ridge overlooking a seasonal waterfall in Tachevah Canyon. It is a short distance down the Museum Trail to a picnic area with a sweeping view of Palm Springs and the Coachella Valley.

Distance: 1.6 miles out and back

Approximate hiking time: 2 hours

Difficulty: Moderate

Trail surface: Dirt and rocks

Best season: Oct through Mar

Water availability: None

Other trail users: Mountain bikes and horses

Canine compatibility: Dogs not allowed

Maps: USGS Palm Springs; Santa Rosa and San Jacinto Mountains National Monument Trail Map

Fees and permits: None

Trail contact: Santa Rosa and San Jacinto Mountains National Monument Visitor Center, 51-500 Highway 74, Palm Desert, CA 92260; (760) 862-9984; www .blm.gov/ca/st/en/fo/palm springs/santarosa.html

Special considerations: During the summer hike early in the day, carry plenty of water, and plan to be finished with the hike by midmorning.

Finding the trailhead: From Palm Springs at the intersection of East Palm Canyon Drive and South Palm Canyon Drive, drive 1 mile north on South Palm Canyon Drive and then turn left on Ramon Road. Continue 0.6 mile to the signed trailhead at the end of the road. GPS: N33° 48.953' W116° 33.340'

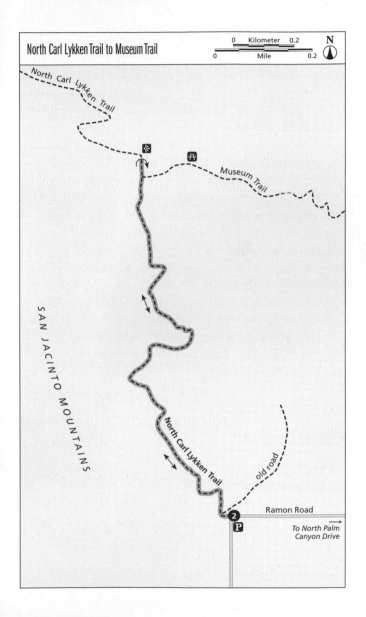

North Carl Lykken Trail to Museum Trail

0 Kilometer 0.2

0 Mile 0.2

N

North Carl Lykken Trail

Museum Trail

SAN JACINTO MOUNTAINS

North Carl Lykken Trail

old road

Ramon Road

2 P

To North Palm Canyon Drive

The Hike

Start on an old road that traverses the mountain slope just above the base, but after a few yards turn left onto the North Carl Lykken Trail, which climbs a series of switchbacks above the old road. When the ascent moderates, follow the trail north across a couple of shallow basins. In the spring after a wet winter, these little basins are alive with wildflowers and green grass. Other plants are typical of this desert area, including creosote bush, mesquite, and cholla cactus.

After crossing the second basin, the North Carl Lykken Trail swings around a ridge and traverses north along the mountainside. The view across Palm Springs is immediate and expansive. Finally, another gradual climb leads north to the junction with the Museum Trail. From here, you can walk a few yards north on the North Carl Lykken Trail to a point overlooking the seasonal waterfall in Tachevah Canyon.

The two Lykken trails, north and south, were named after Carl Lykken, a Palm Springs pioneer who arrived in 1913, ran a general store, and was the town's first postmaster.

Optionally, you can walk 0.1 mile east on the Museum Trail to reach a picnic area nestled in a small basin surrounded by granite boulders.

Miles and Directions

0.0 Start at the trailhead.

0.3 The ascent moderates.

0.7 Reach the ridge.

0.8 Arrive at the junction with Museum Trail; continue north on the North Carl Lykken Trail to the viewpoint. Retrace your steps.

1.6 Arrive back at the trailhead.

3 Museum Trail

The Museum Trail starts from the Palm Springs Art Museum and intercepts the longer North Carl Lykken Trail at about its midpoint. The Museum Trail is a fast but steep way to get to the picnic area on the ridge above the museum, and also the viewpoint just northwest of the picnic area.

Distance: 1.6 miles out and back
Approximate hiking time: 1 hour
Difficulty: Moderate
Trail surface: Dirt and rocks
Best season: Oct through Mar
Water availability: None
Other trail users: None
Canine compatibility: Dogs not allowed
Maps: USGS Palm Springs; Santa Rosa and San Jacinto Mountains National Monument Trail Map

Fees and permits: None
Trail contact: Santa Rosa and San Jacinto Mountains National Monument Visitor Center, 51-500 Highway 74, Palm Desert, CA 92260; (760) 862-9984; www .blm.gov/ca/st/en/fo/palm springs/santarosa.html
Special considerations: During the summer hike early in the day, carry plenty of water, and plan to be finished with the hike by midmorning.

Finding the trailhead: From Palm Springs at the intersection of East Palm Canyon Drive and South Palm Canyon Drive, drive 1.5 miles north on South Palm Canyon Drive, which becomes Indian Canyon Drive, and turn left on East Tahquitz Canyon Way. Drive 0.2 mile, then turn right on North Museum Drive. Drive 0.1 mile and turn left into the museum parking lot. Park at the northwest corner of the parking lot, near the museum trailhead sign. GPS: N33° 49.511' W116° 33.010'

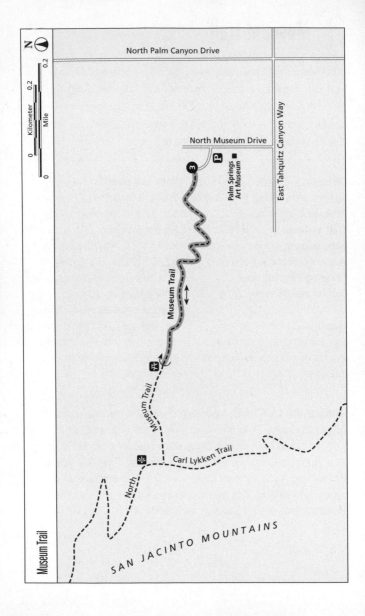

The Hike

This short hike climbs steeply up the ridge directly above the museum, gaining elevation rapidly for some fine views of Palm Springs. Just above the trailhead the trail crosses a private road; stay on the trail here and respect the private land. Steep but well-used switchbacks continue right on up the broad crest of the ridge. When the ascent moderates, you'll reach a small picnic area. Set among piles of granite boulders, the picnic area is a fine place to relax and enjoy the view.

The junction with the North Carl Lykken Trail is 0.1 mile west of the picnic area, and you can continue the hike either north or south on the North Carl Lykken Trail. Just 0.1 mile north of the junction, the North Carl Lykken Trail comes to another fine viewpoint, this one looking north.

Before or after your hike, check out the Palm Springs Art Museum, which features contemporary and Western art, as well as natural history exhibits.

Miles and Directions

0.0 Begin at the Museum Trailhead.

0.8 Arrive at the picnic area on the ridge. Return the way you came.

1.6 Arrive back at the Museum Trailhead.

4 South Carl Lykken Trail-North

Starting from the north end of the South Carl Lykken Trail, you can hike to a point with a view of Tahquitz Falls, and also to a picnic area on the ridge above the falls. Of all the trails in the San Jacinto foothills, this hike offers some of the best views of Palm Springs.

Distance: 4.0 miles out and back
Approximate hiking time: 3 hours
Difficulty: Moderate
Trail surface: Dirt and rocks
Best season: Oct through Mar
Water availability: None
Other trail users: Horses and mountain bikes
Canine compatibility: Dogs not allowed
Maps: USGS Palm Springs; Santa Rosa and San Jacinto Mountains National Monument Trail Map
Fees and permits: None
Trail contact: Santa Rosa and San Jacinto Mountains National Monument Visitor Center, 51-500 Highway 74, Palm Desert, CA 92260; (760) 862-9984; www.blm.gov/ca/st/en/fo/palm springs/santarosa.html
Special considerations: During the summer hike early in the day, carry plenty of water, and plan to be finished with the hike by midmorning.

Finding the trailhead: From Palm Springs at the intersection of East Palm Canyon Drive and South Palm Canyon Drive, drive 0.5 mile north on South Palm Canyon Drive (it becomes Indian Canyon Drive north of East Tahquitz Canyon Way) and then turn left onto Mesquite Avenue. Go 0.2 mile and park on the right. There is no parking at the signed trailhead, 0.2 mile farther west at the end of Mesquite Avenue. GPS: N33° 48.518' W116° 32.854'

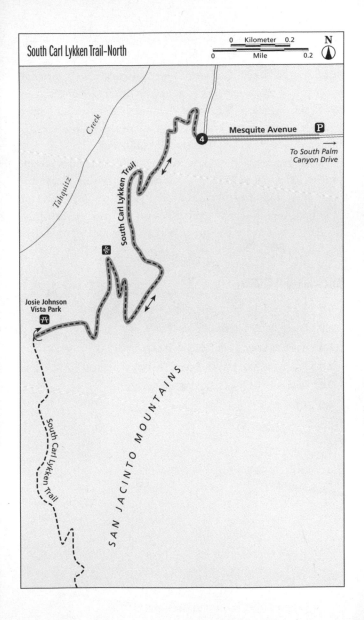

South Carl Lykken Trail-North

0   Kilometer   0.2

0   Mile   0.2

N

Creek

Tahquitz

South Carl Lykken Trail

Mesquite Avenue P

4

To South Palm
Canyon Drive

Josie Johnson
Vista Park

S A N   J A C I N T O   M O U N T A I N S

South Carl Lykken Trail

The Hike

Walk west up the street for 0.2 mile to its end and the South Carl Lykken Trailhead. The trail climbs in a series of switchbacks, working its way generally southwest and staying below the ridgetop. A gradual ascent across the hillside leads to more switchbacks, which in turn emerge on the crest of the ridge at a point overlooking Tahquitz Falls.

After enjoying the view of the falls, continue up the South Carl Lykken Trail as it traverses southwest below the ridge crest and then makes a final climb to Josie Johnson Vista Park, a picnic area with tables on the crest. After enjoying the view (and a picnic, if you brought one), return the way you came.

Miles and Directions

0.0 Start in the parking area along Mesquite Avenue.

0.2 Reach the South Carl Lykken Trailhead.

1.4 Arrive at the view of Tahquitz Falls.

2.0 Reach the picnic area. Return the way you came.

3.8 Return to the South Carl Lykken Trailhead.

4.0 Arrive back at the parking area.

5 South Carl Lykken Trail-South

The south end of the South Carl Lykken Trail offers a longer but gentler climb to the picnic area above Tahquitz Canyon. It offers views of south Palm Springs.

Distance: 5 miles out and back
Approximate hiking time: 3 to 4 hours
Difficulty: Moderate
Trail surface: Dirt and rocks
Best season: Oct through Mar
Water availability: None
Other trail users: Horses and mountain bikes
Canine compatibility: Dogs not allowed
Maps: USGS Palm Springs; Santa Rosa and San Jacinto Mountains National Monument Trail Map

Fees and permits: None
Trail contact: Santa Rosa and San Jacinto Mountains National Monument Visitor Center, 51-500 Highway 74, Palm Desert, CA 92260; (760) 862-9984; www .blm.gov/ca/st/en/fo/palm springs/santarosa.html
Special considerations: During the summer hike early in the day, carry plenty of water, and plan to be finished with the hike by midmorning.

Finding the trailhead: From Palm Springs at the intersection of East Palm Canyon Drive and South Palm Canyon Drive, drive 1.7 miles south on South Palm Canyon Drive and park along either side of the road just south of Murray Canyon Drive. GPS: N33° 46.717' W116° 32.733'

The Hike

The trail follows an old road to the west, just south of a group of houses, and soon turns northwest and heads for the base of the slopes. Several switchbacks take you to the

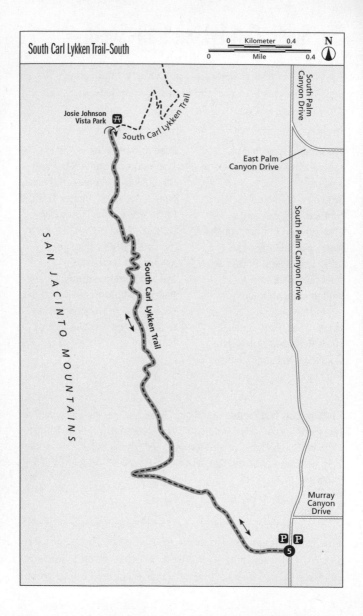

South Carl Lykken Trail-South

0 Kilometer 0.4
0 Mile 0.4

N

Josie Johnson
Vista Park

South Carl Lykken Trail

South Carl Lykken Trail

SAN JACINTO MOUNTAINS

South Palm Canyon Drive

East Palm
Canyon Drive

South Palm Canyon Drive

Murray
Canyon
Drive

P P
5

top of a ridge and a viewpoint with picnic tables. From here the trail heads north along the steep slopes of the lower San Jacintos. A gradual climb with great views along the way finally takes you to Josie Johnson Vista Park, the picnic area overlooking Tahquitz Canyon.

Miles and Directions

0.0 Start at the South Carl Lykken Trailhead.

0.4 The trail starts to climb the steep slope to the north.

0.9 Cross a ridge.

2.5 Reach the picnic area on the ridge above Tahquitz Canyon; return the way you came.

5.0 Arrive back at the South Carl Lykken Trailhead.

6 Garstin-Earl Henderson Loop

This loop hike takes you over a small summit at the northwest end of the Santa Rosa Mountains. It features a fine walk along a ridge with views of the Santa Rosa Mountains and of Palm Springs, and returns along the base of the mountains above Palm Canyon Wash.

Distance: 3.2-mile loop
Approximate hiking time: 2 to 3 hours
Difficulty: Moderate
Trail surface: Dirt and rocks
Best season: Oct through Mar
Water availability: None
Other trail users: Horses
Canine compatibility: Dogs not allowed
Maps: USGS Palm Springs; Santa Rosa and San Jacinto Mountains National Monument Trail Map

Fees and permits: None
Trail contact: Santa Rosa and San Jacinto Mountains National Monument Visitor Center, 51-500 Highway 74, Palm Desert, CA 92260; (760) 862-9984; www .blm.gov/ca/st/en/fo/palm springs/santarosa.html
Special considerations: During the summer hike early in the day, carry plenty of water, and plan to be finished with the hike by midmorning.

Finding the trailhead: From Palm Springs at the intersection of East Palm Canyon Drive and South Palm Canyon Drive, drive south on South Palm Canyon Drive for 1.8 miles and then turn left on Bogert Trail. Drive 0.9 mile and turn left onto Barona Road. Go 0.1 mile to the end of the road and park along the side of the road. GPS: N33° 46.567' W116° 31.883'

The Hike

From the trailhead sign, walk up the trail onto a low ridge just above the street. From here you can see downstream along Palm Canyon Wash, which will be your return route via the Earl Henderson Trail. The trail heads right across the slope and climbs to a trail junction. Earl Henderson Trail goes left. For now, stay right on the Garstin Trail.

A series of well-graded switchbacks allow the trail to gain elevation quickly, and soon you'll pass a BLM sign prohibiting dogs beyond this point. Please respect this closure to protect the endangered peninsular bighorn sheep, which will leave the area if disturbed by dogs.

After more steady climbing with ever-improving views, the Garstin Trail tops out on a scenic ridge and follows this ridge northeast to the Wildhorse Trail junction. Stay left on the Garstin Trail and continue along the ridge to the Shannon Trail. You'll turn left here to continue the loop—but first, walk a few yards on the Berns Trail to an unnamed small summit. This popular spot is the high point on the ridge, and it offers a 360-degree view of Palm Springs to the north and the foothills of the Santa Rosa Mountains to the south and southeast. Westward, the high San Jacinto Mountains dominate the view.

Walk down the Shannon Trail, which descends a ridge to the northeast. Before you reach the base of the mountains, the Shannon Trail ends at a junction with the Earl Henderson Trail. Turn left and follow the Earl Henderson Trail as it more or less contours along the steep slopes just above Palm Canyon Wash. Named after a local horseman who was instrumental in building many of the trails in the Palm Springs area, the Earl Henderson Trail continues above Palm

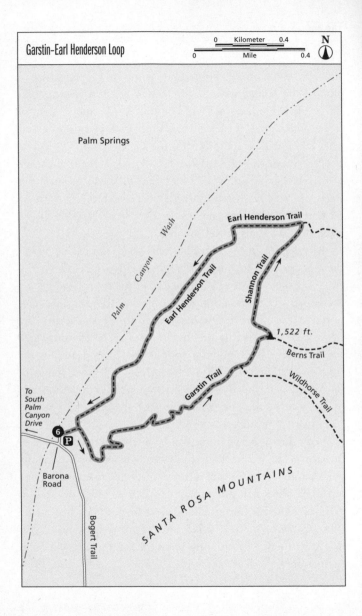

Garstin-Earl Henderson Loop

Palm Springs

Palm Canyon Wash

Earl Henderson Trail

Earl Henderson Trail

Shannon Trail

1,522 ft.

Berns Trail

Wildhorse Trail

Garstin Trail

To South Palm Canyon Drive

6 P

Barona Road

Bogert Trail

SANTA ROSA MOUNTAINS

0 Kilometer 0.4

0 Mile 0.4

N

Canyon Wash until it meets the junction with the Garstin Trail. Turn right and follow the trail a short distance down to the trailhead.

Miles and Directions

0.0 Start at the Earl Henderson Trailhead.

0.1 Arrive at the junction with the Garstin Trail; turn right on Garstin Trail.

1.0 Reach the top of the steep climb.

1.2 At the Wildhorse Trail junction, stay left on the Garstin Trail.

1.4 At the Shannon Trail junction, go left on the Shannon Trail.

1.9 Turn left on the Earl Henderson Trail.

3.1 Turn right to stay on the Earl Henderson Trail.

3.2 Arrive back at the Earl Henderson Trailhead.

Indian Canyons

The Indian Canyons are a series of deep canyons cut into the steep granite slopes of the San Jacinto Mountains as they rise abruptly from the edge of Palm Springs. Several of these canyons are on the reservation lands of the Agua Caliente Band of Cahuilla Indians. Known as the Indian Canyons, these consist of lower Palm Canyon and several of its tributaries, including Andreas and Murray Canyons. Located in south Palm Springs, the Indian Canyons are very easy to reach from the city. Also included in this section is Tahquitz Canyon, on the west side of the city between the North and South Carl Lykken Trails. The tribe operates a visitor center here and provides an enjoyable loop trail in the lower canyon, highlighted by Tahquitz Falls.

7 Tahquitz Canyon Loop

This easy loop in lower Tahquitz Canyon takes you past interesting historical and natural features on the way to Tahquitz Falls.

Distance: 2.1-mile loop
Approximate hiking time: 1 hour
Difficulty: Easy
Trail surface: Dirt and rocks
Best season: Oct through Mar
Water availability: Tahquitz Creek (must be purified)
Other trail users: None
Canine compatibility: Dogs not allowed
Maps: USGS Palm Springs; Santa Rosa and San Jacinto Mountains National Monument

Trail Map; Indian Canyons Trail Guide
Fees and permits: An entrance fee is charged
Trail contact: Agua Caliente Band of Cahuilla Indians; (760) 416-7044; www.tahquitzcanyon .com
Special considerations: During the summer hike early in the day, carry plenty of water, and plan to be finished with the hike by midmorning.

Finding the trailhead: From Palm Springs at the intersection of East Palm Canyon Drive and South Palm Canyon Drive, drive 0.6 mile north on South Palm Canyon Drive (it becomes Indian Canyon Drive north of East Tahquitz Canyon Way) and then turn left on Mesquite Avenue. Continue 0.8 mile to the end of the street and then turn right on the Tahquitz Canyon entrance road. Drive 0.2 mile, passing the visitor center, to the parking lot at the end of the road. GPS: N33° 48.632' W116° 33.112'

The Hike

Starting from the parking lot, walk back up the entrance road to the visitor center. Pay the entrance fee here and pick up a trail brochure. The trail starts from the rear door of the visitor center (there are restrooms here) and heads up the broad fan of outwash debris on the canyon bottom, staying on the left (south) side of Tahquitz Creek.

At a bridged crossing of Tahquitz Creek, the return trail, which is mostly on the south side of the creek, meets the outbound trail. Stay right here, unless you want to take an optional shortcut return. Do the same thing at the second junction with the return loop: Stay right to continue the hike.

You'll soon encounter an old diversion gate, where Tahquitz Creek was once diverted into a ditch and pipeline. The water was used to irrigate fields downstream.

Next you'll pass a U.S. Geological Survey stream gauge, which is on the left. The gauge reports the stream level to a satellite, and information from the national network of stream gauges is used to predict runoff into reservoirs and to warn of flood conditions. Normally, a small dam with a specially shaped pour-off is constructed to create the pool that the stream gauge monitors. This allows the water level to be correlated to the amount of water flowing down the stream. In this case, a handy natural pour-off was used.

Tahquitz Falls is at the head of the loop trail. This pleasant waterfall drops over a granite cliff into a pool at the base, which is popular with ducks. The flow of the fall varies seasonally and is at its highest in the spring, when snowmelt runs down from the high San Jacintos above.

Follow the trail across the creek and then downstream, as the return loop makes its way along the south bank of the creek. Stop for a bit, enjoy the view, and listen for the distinctive, melodic, descending trill of the canyon wren, a bird that favors canyons such as these. You'll again encounter

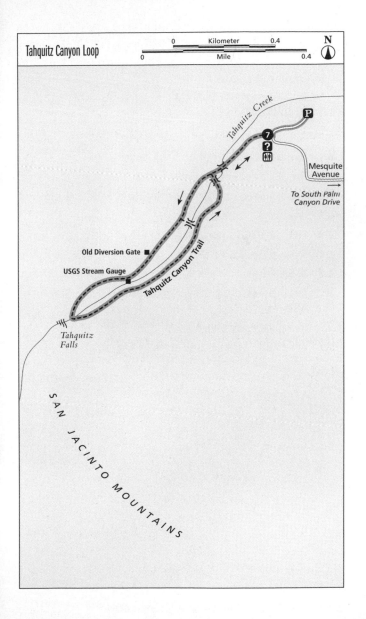

Tahquitz Canyon Loop

Kilometer

0   0.4

Mile

0   0.4

N

Tahquitz Creek

P

7

?

Mesquite Avenue

To South Palm Canyon Drive

Old Diversion Gate

USGS Stream Gauge

Tahquitz Canyon Trail

Tahquitz Falls

SAN JACINTO MOUNTAINS

the two junctions with the outbound trail; stay right at each junction. At the visitor center, walk through the building and then turn left on the entrance road to return to the parking lot and trailhead.

Miles and Directions

0.0 Start at the trailhead at the parking lot.

0.1 Pay the entrance fee at the visitor center.

0.4 Reach the first junction with the return loop; stay right.

0.6 Reach the second junction with the return loop; stay right.

0.7 Pass the old diversion gate.

0.8 Pass the USGS stream gauge.

1.1 Arrive at Tahquitz Falls.

1.5 At the first junction with the outbound loop, stay right.

1.7 Reach the second junction with the outbound loop; stay right.

2.0 Reach the visitor center.

2.1 Arrive back at the trailhead at the parking lot.

8 Andreas Canyon Loop

The Andreas Canyon Trail loops along a permanent creek past many small cascades, under the shade of a large palm oasis. This is a great place for a leisurely hike and a picnic.

Distance: 1-mile loop
Approximate hiking time: 1 hour
Difficulty: Easy
Trail surface: Dirt and rocks
Best season: Oct through Mar
Water availability: Andreas Creek (must be purified)
Other trail users: None
Canine compatibility: Dogs not allowed
Maps: USGS Palm Springs; Santa Rosa and San Jacinto Mountains National Monument

Trail Map; Indian Canyons Trail Guide
Fees and permits: An entrance fee is charged
Trail contact: Agua Caliente Band of Cahuilla Indians; (760) 323-6018; www.indian-canyons .com
Special considerations: During the summer hike early in the day, carry plenty of water, and plan to be finished with the hike by midmorning.

Finding the trailhead: From Palm Springs at the intersection of East Palm Canyon Drive and South Palm Canyon Drive, drive 2.5 miles south on South Palm Canyon Drive to the Indian Canyons entrance station. After paying the entrance fee, continue 0.3 mile and then turn right on Andreas Canyon Road. Continue 0.8 mile to the end of the road and park in the first parking lot/picnic area. GPS: N33° 45.650' W116° 32.966'

The Hike

The loop hike starts at a signed trailhead in the first parking lot and follows the right (north) side of Andreas Creek upstream. This permanent stream graces an outstanding palm

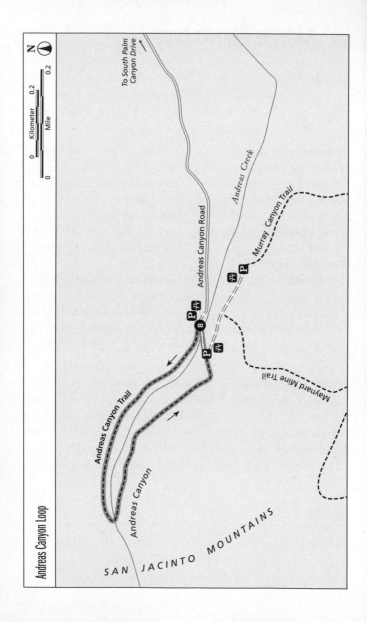

Andreas Canyon Loop

N

Kilometer
0   0.2

Mile
0   0.2

To South Palm Canyon Drive

Andreas Canyon Road

Andreas Creek

Murray Canyon Trail/

Maynard Mine Trail

8

Andreas Canyon Trail

Andreas Canyon

SAN JACINTO MOUNTAINS

oasis. Small cascades add to the pleasant, cool atmosphere. More than 150 species of plants call this shady refuge home, including western sycamores, whose broad leaves provide plenty of summer shade. Also watch for rock metates, round holes in the granite bedrock where Native Americans used stone pestles to grind seeds into flour centuries ago.

The native palm trees that grow along Andreas Creek and in other palm oases in southeastern California are California fan palms. These palms have very thick trunks and grow slowly, living as long as 150 to 200 years. Dead leaves hang vertically down the trunk and unfortunately, catch fire easily. The common planted palm of the desert cities is the Mexican fan palm, which is native to Baja California. Its thin trunk grows quickly and can be twice as tall as the California fan palm.

Miles and Directions

0.0 Start at the Andreas Canyon Trailhead in the first parking lot.

0.5 Reach the upper end of the loop hike at a fence.

0.9 The return trail ends in the second parking lot/picnic area. Follow the road back to the first parking lot.

1.0 Arrive back at the Andreas Canyon Trailhead in the first parking lot.

9 Seven Falls

This hike uses the Murray Canyon Trail to reach a series of waterfalls and cascades in Murray Canyon. Along the way, you'll pass through several palm oases.

Distance: 3.8 miles out and back
Approximate hiking time: 3 hours
Difficulty: Easy
Trail surface: Dirt and rocks
Best season: Oct through Mar
Water availability: Murray Creek (must be purified)
Other trail users: Horses on the first section of the trail
Canine compatibility: Dogs not allowed
Maps: USGS Palm Springs and Palm View Peak; Santa Rosa and San Jacinto Mountains National Monument Trail Map; Indian Canyons Trail Guide
Fees and permits: An entrance fee is charged
Trail contact: Agua Caliente Band of Cahuilla Indians; (760) 323-6018; www.indian-canyons .com
Special considerations: During the summer hike early in the day, carry plenty of water, and plan to be finished with the hike by midmorning.

Finding the trailhead: From Palm Springs at the intersection of East Palm Canyon Drive and South Palm Canyon Drive, drive 2.5 miles south on South Palm Canyon Drive to the Indian Canyons entrance station. After paying the entrance fee, continue 0.3 mile, then turn right on Andreas Canyon Road. Continue 0.8 mile to the end of the paved road, turn left in the first parking area and cross Andreas Creek, then drive through the second parking area to the third and last parking area. GPS: N33° 45.577' W116° 32.866'

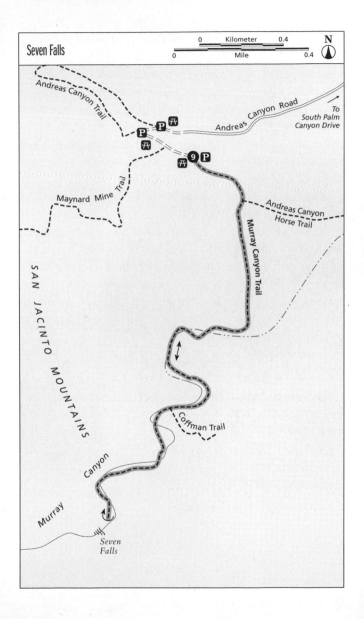

The Hike

From the signed trailhead in the third parking and picnic area, the Murray Canyon Trail heads southeast along the base of the foothills. After encountering the Andreas Canyon Horse Trail (stay right here), the Murray Canyon Trail heads south toward Murray Canyon and crosses the outwash plain at the foot of the mountains to reach the canyon. The trail turns left and follows the creek upstream through a fine palm oasis.

The Coffman Trail, entering from the left, marks the limit of horse travel. The Murray Canyon Trail continues to follow the creek upstream, crossing several times and wandering among big boulders, until it reaches Seven Falls, a series of falls and cascades. You can get a better view of some of the upper falls by climbing up the right (north) slopes a short distance. When you've finished enjoying the falls, return the way you came.

Miles and Directions

0.0 Start at the trailhead in the third parking lot.

0.3 Pass the Andreas Canyon Horse Trail on the left; stay right on the Murray Canyon Trail.

0.6 Enter Murray Canyon.

1.3 Pass the Coffman Trail on the left; stay right on the Murray Canyon Trail.

1.9 Arrive at Seven Falls; return the way you came.

3.8 Arrive back at the trailhead.

10 Maynard Mine Trail

A long climb up the ridge between Andreas and Murray Canyons leads to a scenic point and the old Maynard Mine.

Distance: 4.4 miles out and back
Approximate hiking time: 3 to 4 hours
Difficulty: Moderate
Trail surface: Dirt and rocks
Best season: Oct through Mar
Water availability: None
Other trail users: Horses
Canine compatibility: Dogs not allowed
Maps: USGS Palm Springs and Palm View Peak; Santa Rosa and San Jacinto Mountains National Monument Trail Map; Indian Canyons Trail Guide
Fees and permits: An entrance fee is charged
Trail contact: Agua Caliente Band of Cahuilla Indians; (760) 323-6018; www.indian-canyons .com
Special considerations: During the summer hike early in the day, carry plenty of water, and plan to be finished with the hike by midmorning.

Finding the trailhead: From Palm Springs at the intersection of East Palm Canyon Drive and South Palm Canyon Drive, drive 2.5 miles south on South Palm Canyon Drive to the Indian Canyons entrance station. After paying the entrance fee, continue 0.3 mile, then turn right on Andreas Canyon Road. Continue 0.8 mile to the end of the road and park in the second parking lot/picnic area, to the left across Andreas Creek. GPS: N33° 45.613' W116° 32.963'

The Hike

Pick up the Maynard Mine Trail at the signed trailhead on the south side of the second parking lot. The trail climbs out onto the slopes above Andreas Canyon and starts a steady

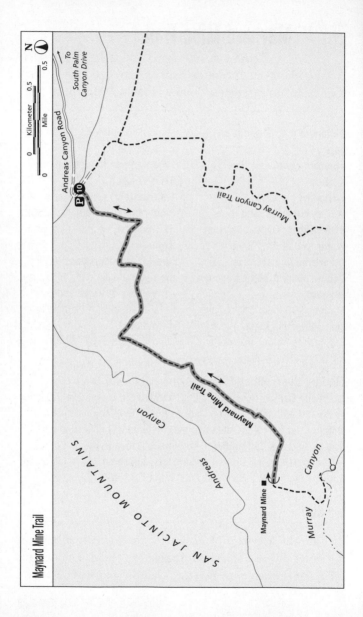

Maynard Mine Trail

climb to the west. Several switchbacks finally lead to the top of the ridge between Andreas and Murray Canyons.

The Maynard Mine Trail follows this ridge more or less west and continues the steady climb to a hill, which is the high point of the hike. The trail then descends to a saddle and the site of the old Maynard Mine. Tungsten, a very hard and dense steel-gray metal, was mined here during World War II. Portugal was the main source before the war, and because the supply was uncertain, American deposits of the two primary tungsten minerals, wolframite and scheelite, were exploited during the war years. Tungsten is a vital component of metal alloys and is also used in electrical and electronic components such as incandescent lightbulbs and X-ray tubes.

Return the way you came. Optionally, you can hike south, continuing down the trail to reach Murray Canyon and a seasonal spring. This point is well upstream of Seven Falls.

Miles and Directions

0.0 Start at the Maynard Mine Trailhead in the second parking area.

1.0 The trail reaches the ridge crest and the first views of Andreas Canyon.

1.6 Reach the high point of the trail.

2.2 Arrive at Maynard Mine below the saddle; return the way you came.

4.4 Arrive back at the trailhead.

11 Victor Loop

This gorgeous loop takes in the segment of Palm Canyon containing the world's largest California fan palm oasis, as well as a desert ridgetop trail featuring close views of the palm oasis and distant views of the surrounding Santa Rosa and San Jacinto Mountains. There are many connecting trails, which allow options for longer day hikes. This loop hike is described in a counterclockwise direction, which is perfect for cool weather. In warm weather, you may prefer to do the loop in reverse, so that you hike the exposed Victor Trail along the shadeless ridge before the day heats up, and then return under the shade of the palms along Palm Canyon.

Distance: 3-mile loop
Approximate hiking time: 2 hours
Difficulty: Easy
Trail surface: Dirt and rocks
Best season: Oct through Mar
Water availability: Palm Canyon Creek (must be purified before use)
Other trail users: Horses
Canine compatibility: Dogs not allowed
Maps: USGS Palm View Peak; Santa Rosa and San Jacinto

Mountains National Monument Trail Map; Indian Canyons Trail Guide
Fees and permits: An entrance fee is charged
Trail contact: Agua Caliente Band of Cahuilla Indians; (760) 323-6018; www.indian-canyons .com
Special considerations: During the summer hike early in the day, carry plenty of water, and plan to be finished with the hike by midmorning.

Finding the trailhead: From Palm Springs at the intersection of East Palm Canyon Drive and South Palm Canyon Drive, drive 2.5 miles south on South Palm Canyon Drive to the Indian Canyons entrance station. Pay the entrance fee and pick up a trail map. Continue 2.1 miles to the end of the road at the Trading Post. GPS: N33° 44.274' W116° 32.311'

The Hike

Visit the small Trading Post for snacks, cold drinks, and souvenirs either before or after your hike. The loop hike starts with the Palm Canyon Trail, which leaves the parking lot immediately to the left of the Trading Post and descends into Palm Canyon.

Once at the bottom of the canyon, the Palm Canyon Trail turns right and wanders upstream through a picnic area before crossing Palm Canyon Creek and heading generally south. You'll pass the turnoff to the West Fork Trail; continue straight ahead on the Palm Canyon Trail. At least in the spring, the creek has a good flow, and complements the sound of the wind and birdsong in the palm tops high overhead.

All too soon, you'll leave the creek behind as the Palm Canyon Trail turns left up the East Fork of Palm Canyon. Turn left on the Victor Trail, which climbs out of the canyon, and then almost immediately turn sharply left again, to remain on the Victor Trail at the junction with the East Fork and Vandeventer Trails.

Follow the Victor Trail north as it climbs onto the ridge just east of Palm Canyon. After the confines of the palm-shaded canyon, the open views from the ridge are stunning. Much of the northern Santa Rosa Mountains are visible, as are the east slopes of the San Jacinto Mountains, from the 10,000-foot summits to the flat valley containing Palm Springs.

Barrel cactus is common along the Victor Trail. These short, squat cacti have a broad, shallow root system that is very effective at collecting moisture from the soil after rare desert rains. The plant stores this moisture in its fleshy interior, which is surrounded by vertical, woody staves. As the plant takes in moisture, the staves are free to move apart as the accordion-shaped pleats of the skin expand. The skin of the barrel cactus is tough and waxy, which inhibits moisture loss due to evaporation. A nest of interlocking sharp spines discourages animals and birds from dining on the succulent interior.

A common desert myth is that you can get water from the barrel cactus in an emergency. Unfortunately, it's not true. First of all, you'd need an ax or machete to get through the plant's defenses, and then all you'd have is a bitter pulp, which would hardly be worth the effort and the sweat you'd expend getting to it. Better to search for water holes along the canyon bottoms—or even better, to carry and drink enough water.

As the Trading Post comes into view, the Victor Trail descends off the north end of the ridge and meets the Fern Canyon and Alexander Trails at a four-way intersection. Turn sharply left, toward the Trading Post. After the trail crosses Palm Canyon Creek, follow the stream up to the overflow parking lot and then along the short connecting road to the main parking lot and the trailhead at the Trading Post.

Options: There are many trails in the area of lower Palm Canyon and its tributaries, which may be used for day hikes as well as backpack trips. Refer to the Santa Rosa and San Jacinto Mountains National Monument Trail Map or Indian Canyons Trail Guide for information.

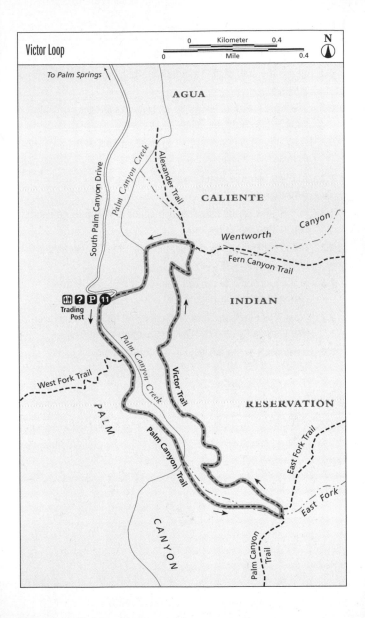

Victor Loop

To Palm Springs

AGUA

South Palm Canyon Drive

Palm Canyon Creek

Alexander Trail

CALIENTE

Canyon

Wentworth

Fern Canyon Trail

Trading Post

11

INDIAN

West Fork Trail

Palm Canyon Creek

Victor Trail

PALM

RESERVATION

Palm Canyon Trail

East Fork Trail

East Fork

CANYON

Palm Canyon Trail

Kilometer

Mile

N

Miles and Directions

0.0   Begin at the trailhead at the Trading Post.

0.1   Reach the start of the Palm Canyon Trail; turn right and hike upstream.

0.3   The West Fork Trail leaves the canyon on the right; continue straight ahead on the Palm Canyon Trail.

0.8   Follow the Palm Canyon Trail up the East Fork of Palm Canyon.

1.2   Turn left onto the Victor Trail, which climbs out of the canyon.

1.3   At the junction the East Fork and Vandeventer Trails go right; stay left on the Victor Trail.

2.3   The Victor Trail descends from the ridge; the Trading Post is visible across Palm Canyon.

2.5   At the junction with the Fern Canyon and Alexander Trails, turn left toward the Trading Post.

2.7   Cross Palm Canyon Creek and follow the trail up to the overflow parking lot, and then left to the main parking lot.

3.0   Arrive back at the trailhead at the Trading Post.

Palms to Pines

CA 74, the Palms to Pines Highway, connects the desert cities of the Coachella Valley to the high country of the Santa Rosa and San Jacinto Mountains. Although the highest mountain areas are beyond the scope of this book, there are several hikes within less than an hour's drive that lie at intermediate elevations and offer a change of scenery as well as a break from the desert heat.

12 Art Smith Trail

The Art Smith Trail connects CA 74, the Palms to Pines Highway, with Dunn Road, climbing the east slopes of the Santa Rosa Mountains. A palm oasis hidden deep in the mountains is the goal for this hike, which is on the eastern section of the trail.

Distance: 4.4 miles out and back
Approximate hiking time: 3 hours
Difficulty: Moderate
Trail surface: Dirt and rocks
Best season: Oct through Mar
Water availability: None
Other trail users: Horses and mountain bikes
Canine compatibility: Dogs not allowed
Maps: USGS Rancho Mirage; Santa Rosa and San Jacinto Mountains National Monument Trail Map

Fees and permits: None. A free permit will be required in the future.
Trail contact: Santa Rosa and San Jacinto Mountains National Monument Visitor Center, 51-500 Highway 74, Palm Desert, CA 92260; (760) 862-9984; www .blm.gov/ca/st/en/fo/palm springs/santarosa.html
Special considerations: During the summer hike early in the day, carry plenty of water, and plan to be finished with the hike by midmorning.

Finding the trailhead: From Palm Springs at the intersection of East Palm Canyon Drive and South Palm Canyon Drive, drive 11.2 miles east on East Palm Canyon Drive and then turn right onto CA 74, the Palms to Pines Highway. Continue 3.9 miles to the Art Smith Trailhead, which is on the right, just past the Santa Rosa and San Jacinto Mountains National Monument Visitor Center turnoff. GPS: N33° 40.084' W116° 24.500'

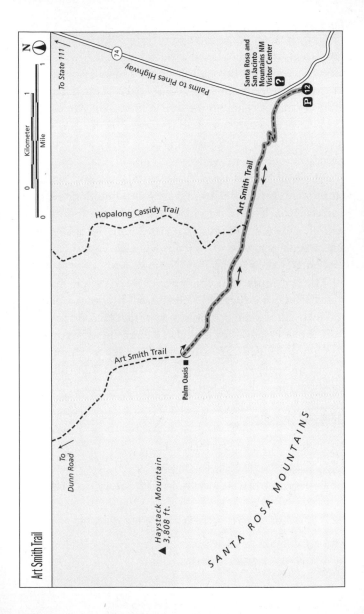

The Hike

From the trailhead, head north and then follow the base of the levee across the mouth of the canyon. At the north end of the levee, follow the edge of the wash north for a short distance to pick up the trail climbing the slopes to the right. Several switchbacks lead to a view to the north along the foothills. The Art Smith Trail now heads west, climbing steadily as it works its way through granite outcrops.

The trail climbs up a ridge to the junction with the Hopalong Cassidy Trail, named after the famous movie cowboy character. This trail heads north across the foothills, but stay left on the Art Smith Trail. Art Smith, the trail's namesake, was the trail boss of a local riding club, and was a tireless advocate for trails in the Palm Springs area.

The Art Smith Trail continues to work its way generally west through the rugged foothills, until it crosses a drainage and then follows the northeast side of the drainage to a palm oasis, the destination for the hike. Return the way you came.

Optionally, you can continue 4.1 miles to Dunn Road (closed to vehicles). Return as you came for a 12.6-mile out-and-back hike. Allow a full day for this option.

Miles and Directions

0.0 Begin at the Art Smith Trailhead.

0.6 Reach the top of the switchbacks.

1.2 Reach the junction with the Hopalong Cassidy Trail; stay left on the Art Smith Trail.

2.2 Arrive at the palm oasis. Return the way you came.

4.4 Arrive back at the trailhead.

13 Randall Henderson Loop

A short but interesting loop through the desert foothills near the Santa Rosa and San Jacinto Mountains National Monument Visitor Center.

Distance: 1.7-mile loop
Approximate hiking time: 1 hour
Difficulty: Easy
Trail surface: Dirt and rocks
Best season: Oct through Mar
Water availability: None
Other trail users: Mountain bikes
Canine compatibility: Dogs not allowed
Maps: USGS Rancho Mirage; Santa Rosa and San Jacinto Mountains National Monument Trail Map

Fees and permits: None
Trail contact: Santa Rosa and San Jacinto Mountains National Monument Visitor Center, 51-500 Highway 74, Palm Desert, CA 92260; (760) 862-9984; www .blm.gov/ca/st/en/fo/palm springs/santarosa.html
Special considerations: During the summer hike early in the day, carry plenty of water, and plan to be finished with the hike by midmorning.

Finding the trailhead: From Palm Springs at the intersection of East Palm Canyon Drive and South Palm Canyon Drive, drive 11.2 miles east on East Palm Canyon Drive and then turn right onto CA 74, the Palms to Pines Highway. Continue 3.8 miles to the Santa Rosa and San Jacinto Mountains National Monument Visitor Center turnoff, on the left. GPS: N33° 40.250' W116° 24.517'

The Hike

From the signed trailhead at the bend in the visitor center access road, follow the Randall Henderson Trail across the open desert to a junction marking the start of the loop. Stay right to begin the loop. There are several hiker-made trails along the loop—stay on the main trail in each case.

The Randall Henderson Trail works its way east along a ridge just south of a minor drainage. A junction marks the cutoff trail, which shortcuts the loop—stay right to stay on the main trail. Near the high point of the loop, two unsigned trails fork right and climb to a road above the trail; stay left to stay on the Randall Henderson Trail.

Common spring flowers along the Randall Henderson Trail include scarlet Indian paintbrush, yellow brittlebush, and red tularosa. If you're really lucky, you may see some of the showy flowers of the otherwise unremarkable hedgehog cactus. This low, small cactus is easily overlooked—until it blooms.

Teddy bear, or jumping, cholla is common here. This cuddly-looking cactus has a dense mass of sharp yellow spines on its stems. The ends of the stems, or joints, are fragile and easily break off. Like many of the other chollas, the spines are microscopically barbed and the plant reproduces by hitching a ride on any hiker or animal foolish enough to brush up against it. The spines attach so easily that some people swear the ball-shaped joints must have jumped onto them, hence the alternate name. Even lightly imbedded joints take a pair of sticks to remove. It's best to have someone else do this maneuver, and it hurts less if the joint is removed suddenly. Just be sure the cactus ball isn't flicked onto someone else. Individual spines are best removed with tweezers, but deeply embedded spines may require a doctor visit. Also, check the ground before sitting down. Old cholla balls turn gray and blend into the ground very nicely.

As it starts to descend, the Randall Henderson Trail drops into the wash and follows it downstream past the cutoff trail

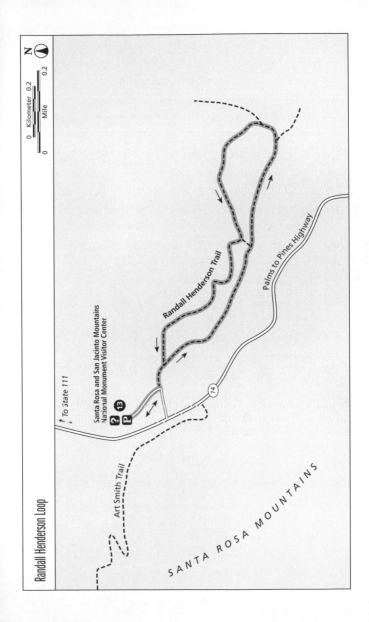

Randall Henderson Loop

N

0   Kilometer   0.2

0   Mile   0.2

To State 111

Santa Rosa and San Jacinto Mountains
National Monument Visitor Center

P   13

Randall Henderson Trail

Palms to Pines Highway

74

Art Smith Trail

SANTA ROSA MOUNTAINS

junction. Stay right to remain on the main trail. For a short distance, the trail runs through a narrows in the canyon walls, then meets the junction at the end of the loop portion. Stay right to follow the trail back to the trailhead on the visitor center road.

Randall Henderson was the editor of *Desert Magazine* and also founded the Desert Protective Council in 1954, which is still actively working to protect the deserts of the Southwest.

Miles and Directions

0.0 Start at the visitor center and walk southeast along the road to the signed Randall Henderson Trailhead.

0.1 Turn east on the Randall Henderson Trail.

0.2 At the start of the loop trail, stay right.

0.7 The shortcut trail forks left; stay right.

0.9 Two unmarked trails branch right; stay left on the Randall Henderson Trail at each junction.

1.3 The shortcut trail goes left; stay right.

1.5 Reach the end of the loop trail; stay right.

1.7 Arrive back at the Randall Henderson Trailhead.

14 Upper Palm Canyon

Palm Canyon is long, beginning in the pinyon-juniper woodland just north of CA 74, the Palms to Pines Highway. This hike follows a lightly used trail into the headwaters of the seasonal stream in upper Palm Canyon, and offers views of the Palm Canyon drainage and all of the surrounding mountains.

Distance: 3.4 miles out and back
Approximate hiking time: 2 to 3 hours
Difficulty: Easy
Trail surface: Dirt and rocks
Best season: Oct through Mar
Water availability: Palm Canyon stream (must be purified)
Other trail users: Horses and mountain bikes
Canine compatibility: Leashed dogs permitted
Maps: USGS Toro Peak and Butterfly Peak; Santa Rosa and San Jacinto Mountains National Monument Trail Map
Fees and permits: None
Trail contact: Santa Rosa and San Jacinto Mountains National Monument Visitor Center, 51-500 Highway 74, Palm Desert, CA 92260; (760) 862-9984; www .blm.gov/ca/st/en/fo/palm springs/santarosa.html
Special considerations: During the summer hike early in the day, carry plenty of water, and plan to be finished with the hike by midmorning.

Finding the trailhead: From Palm Springs at the intersection of East Palm Canyon Drive and South Palm Canyon Drive, drive 11.2 miles east on East Palm Canyon Drive and then turn right onto CA 74, the Palms to Pines Highway. Continue 18.2 miles to Pine View Drive. Turn right and drive 0.2 mile to the unsigned trailhead at the end of the paved road. GPS: N33° 34.333' W116° 30.050'

The Hike

The Palm Canyon Trail follows an old road northward through the mixed pinyon pine, juniper, and chaparral. Chaparral is a mixture of several brushy plants, and the composition varies from location to location. Here in the headwaters of Palm Canyon, the chaparral includes scrub oak, manzanita, and mountain mahogany. Regardless of the composition, the evergreen brush is a pain for hikers trying to walk cross-country, but provides vital cover for wildlife. Other plants include yucca, with its narrow, sharp-tipped leaves, and the ubiquitous prickly pear cactus. Both of these plants were important resources for the natives, who used the roots of the yucca to make soap, and the long fibrous leaves to make thread. Prickly pear bears a purplish fruit, which can be roasted or made into jelly. In good years, singleleaf pinyon pine bears a tasty and nutritious pine nut, which is popular among Southwestern cooks.

Broad switchbacks descend gradually into the headwaters of Palm Canyon, affording occasional views, but the best viewpoint comes just before the trail starts a steep descent. This point makes a good turnaround for those desiring an easy hike. Here, you're looking at the high San Jacinto Mountains to the northwest, down Palm Canyon to the Little San Bernardino Mountains and Joshua Tree National Park to the north, and at the Santa Rosa Mountains to the northeast, east, and southeast.

After the viewpoint, the Palm Canyon Trail drops down steep ridges to a four-way trail junction. An unsigned old road comes in from the right; the trail straight ahead is the horse trail bypass, which parallels Palm Canyon on the right. Turn left on the foot trail down into Palm Canyon. Note

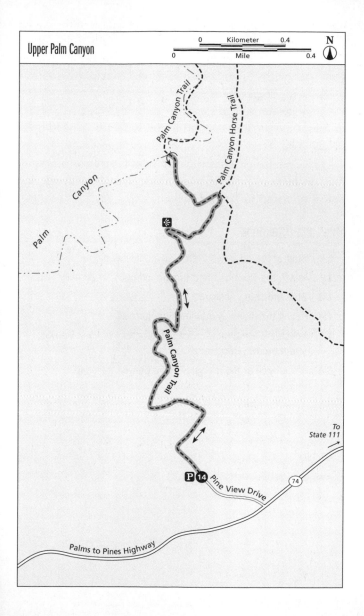

Upper Palm Canyon

0 Kilometer 0.4

0 Mile 0.4

N

Palm Canyon Trail

Palm Canyon Horse Trail

Palm Canyon

Palm

Palm Canyon Trail

To State 111

P 14 Pine View Drive

74

Palms to Pines Highway

how the pinyon pines grow taller and straighter in the cooler, moister environment provided by this north-facing slope. This area is a good example of a microclimate, a relatively small area with a significantly different climate than nearby south-facing slopes.

A moderate descent leads to the little creek in the bed of Palm Canyon. This delightful spot is the turnaround point for the hike.

There are many options in the Palm Canyon area, including the obvious one of a multiday, shuttle backpack trip down the length of Palm Canyon.

Miles and Directions

0.0 Start at the unsigned Palm Canyon trailhead.

1.1 Reach the viewpoint and turnaround point for an easy hike.

1.2 Start the steep descent.

1.4 Reach the four-way trail junction; turn left.

1.7 Reach the turnaround point in the bottom of Palm Canyon; return the way you came.

3.4 Arrive back at the unsigned Palm Canyon trailhead.

15 Cactus Spring Trail

This scenic trail winds through a mix of pinyon pine, juniper, and chaparral past an abandoned gypsum mine to Horsethief Canyon, a wilderness canyon with a seasonal stream. It's a good introduction to the Santa Rosa Wilderness.

Distance: 4.8 miles out and back
Approximate hiking time: 3 to 4 hours
Difficulty: Moderate
Trail surface: Dirt and rocks
Best season: Oct through Mar
Water availability: Horsethief Canyon stream (must be purified)
Other trail users: Horses
Canine compatibility: Leashed dogs permitted
Maps: USGS Toro Peak; Santa Rosa and San Jacinto Mountains National Monument Trail Map

Fees and permits: None
Trail contact: Santa Rosa and San Jacinto Mountains National Monument Visitor Center, 51-500 Highway 74, Palm Desert, CA 92260; (760) 862-9984; www.blm.gov/ca/st/en/fo/palm springs/santarosa.html
Special considerations: During the summer hike early in the day, carry plenty of water, and plan to be finished with the hike by midmorning.

Finding the trailhead: From Palm Springs at the intersection of East Palm Canyon Drive and South Palm Canyon Drive, drive 11.2 miles east on East Palm Canyon Drive and then turn right onto CA 74, the Palms to Pines Highway. Continue 15.4 miles and then turn left on Pinyon Flats Transfer Station Road, which is signed for the Sawmill Trailhead. Continue 0.3 mile to the trailhead at the end of the road. GPS: N33° 34.800' W116° 27.017'

The Hike

Starting from the paved trailhead parking lot, the Cactus Spring Trail follows a dirt road east through the pinyon pine-juniper woodland. It crosses an old road (the Sawmill Trail); continue straight ahead. You'll soon reach a fork where the old road continues straight but the foot trail branches right. Follow the foot trail right as it works its way down into a drainage, and cross the creek for the first time. The Cactus Spring Trail then climbs the far side of this small canyon to pass the remains of an old mine.

After passing the mine, the trail continues east, descending gradually. After crossing another, larger side canyon, the Cactus Spring Trail climbs over a saddle. Descending again, the trail crosses the deepest of the three canyons before climbing over a final saddle and dropping into Horsethief Canyon. The canyon is lined with riparian trees and is a pleasant spot to have lunch before heading back up the trail.

Buckhorn cholla cactus is common along the trail. So-named because the plant's many branches resembles the antlers of a buck deer, this common cactus is found throughout the Mohave and Sonoran deserts. Its spines are short and sparsely distributed along the stems, but the many branches of different lengths create a tangled mass that is effective in defending the plant against would-be munchers. In the spring, buckhorn cholla produces stunning red flowers.

Option: The Cactus Spring Trail can be followed east to Cactus Spring and beyond. It eventually connects to the Boo Hoff Trail via the Guadalupe Trail near La Quinta, and can be used for long shuttle day hikes or a multiday backpack trip.

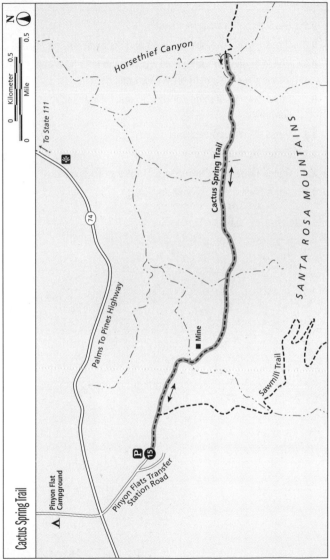

Cactus Spring Trail

N

0   Kilometer   0.5

0   Mile   0.5

To State 111

Pinyon Flat
Campground

Palms To Pines Highway

74

Horsethief Canyon

Cactus Spring Trail

Mine

SANTA ROSA MOUNTAINS

Sawmill Trail

P 15

Pinyon Flats Transfer
Station Road

Miles and Directions

0.0 Start at the Sawmill Trailhead.

0.2 Cross a road (the Sawmill Trail) and continue straight ahead.

0.3 Reach a junction with an old road on the left and a foot trail on the right. Stay right on the foot trail.

0.7 Cross the first of three canyons to reach an abandoned gypsum mine.

1.1 Cross the second canyon.

1.7 Cross the third canyon.

2.4 Reach Horsethief Canyon; return the way you came.

4.8 Arrive back at the Sawmill Trailhead.

North of Palm Springs

Still with an hour's drive of Palm Springs are the north side of the San Jacinto Mountains and the west end of the Little San Bernardino Mountains. The north slopes of the San Jacintos feature one of the most impressive elevation drops found along the Pacific Crest National Scenic Trail, followed by a steep climb into the San Gorgonio Mountains. A hike to an isolated palm oasis provides sweeping views of this area. And a nature preserve along Big Morongo Canyon, with marshlands at its head, provides a unique opportunity to hike through a riparian environment.

16 Vargas Palms

This hike crosses the desert flats north of the San Jacinto Mountains to reach an isolated palm oasis. Highlights included superb views of the dramatic rise from San Gorgonio Pass to the summits of the San Jacintos, and views of the more distant San Gorgonio Mountains. This hike is best done on weekdays when illegal off-road vehicles are not present. The BLM is planning to fence the area to prevent vehicle access.

Distance: 4.6 miles out and back
Approximate hiking time: 2 to 3 hours
Difficulty: Easy
Trail surface: Sand and dirt, with some boulder scrambling
Best season: Oct through Mar
Water availability: None
Other trail users: Off-road vehicles (not legally permitted in this area)
Canine compatibility: Leashed dogs permitted
Map: USGS White Water

Fees and permits: None
Trail contact: Santa Rosa and San Jacinto Mountains National Monument Visitor Center, 51-500 Highway 74, Palm Desert, CA 92260; (760) 862-9984; www.blm.gov/ca/st/en/fo/palm springs/santarosa.html
Special considerations: During the summer hike early in the day, carry plenty of water, and plan to be finished with the hike by midmorning.

Finding the trailhead: From Palm Springs at the intersection of East Palm Canyon Drive and South Palm Canyon Drive, drive 3.1 miles north on North Palm Canyon Drive, which becomes Indian Canyon Drive; turn left at Vista Chino Drive and then right onto North Palm Canyon Drive (CA 111). Continue 8.7 miles and then turn left on Snow Creek Road. Drive 0.4 mile and park on the shoulder of the road, clear of the pavement. There is no formal trailhead. Do not park in Snow Creek Village. GPS: N33° 54.573' W116° 40.268'

The Hike

Though there is no formal trailhead or trail, and the route crosses an area with a maze of off-road vehicle roads and routes, your destination, Vargas Palms, is visible the entire way. This hike is most enjoyable on a cool weekday, when you'll probably have it to yourself.

After parking along Snow Creek Road at the 0.4-mile point (or using the GPS coordinates provided above), look for Vargas Palms nestled in a ravine just above the base of the mountain to the southeast. (If you do have a GPS, save a waypoint at your vehicle before leaving it.) These directions follow old two-track roads to the short trail leading to the palms, but there are many side roads. If you lose the route as described, just head for the ravine to the right of the palms, and you'll get there.

Follow an old two-track road leading southeast, toward the palms. After less than a mile, you'll come to the broad, sandy, and mostly dry wash of the San Gorgonio River. Cross the wash directly toward an old road that ascends a sand hill on the far bank. At the top of this sand hill, look for an old pipeline, the remains of an aqueduct.

Turn right and follow the old pipeline southwest 0.4 mile to an old road that crosses the pipeline at right angles. Turn left and follow this road toward the ravine right of the palms. If you are on the correct road, it will end at a turnaround at the mouth of the right-hand ravine. From here, follow an informal trail up the ravine toward the palms. The last hundred-dred yards or so of this trail winds through granite boulders and may require a bit of rock scrambling.

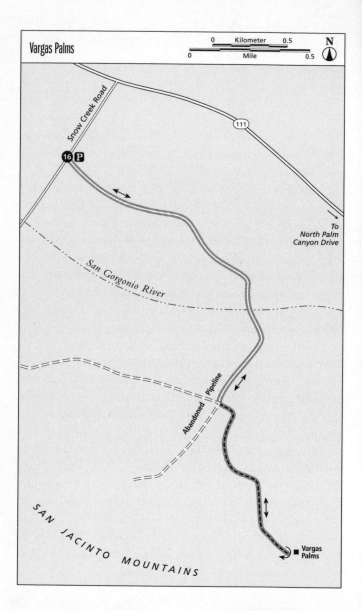

Vargas Palms has very little surface water—an attempt has been made to dig out one of the springs to increase the flow. The view across the valley to the San Gorgonio Mountains through the fronds of the palms alone is worth the hike.

To return, retrace your steps. If you lose your way among the confusion of side roads, just head directly for the right end of Snow Creek Road, and you'll see your vehicle across the open desert as you get closer. If you used a GPS to mark the location of your vehicle, you can use the GPS to walk directly back. The desert plain is easy walking.

Miles and Directions

0.0 Begin at the unsigned starting point on Snow Creek Road.

0.9 Reach the bank of the San Gorgonio River bed; cross the riverbed toward an old road that climbs a sand hill.

1.1 On the far bank of the San Gorgonio River bed, follow an old aqueduct pipeline right (southwest).

1.5 Leave the old aqueduct pipeline and hike southeast toward the drainage right of the palms.

1.9 Where the old road ends, follow an informal trail into the drainage right of the palms.

2.1 Ascend the drainage to the palms.

2.3 Vargas Palms. Return the way you came.

4.6 Arrive back at the unsigned starting point on Snow Creek Road.

17 Big Morongo Canyon

Part of the Big Morongo Canyon Preserve, the trail down Big Morongo Canyon takes you through a wild and scenic canyon that cuts through the western end of the Little San Bernardino Mountains. The canyon is prime desert bighorn sheep habitat, and if you're lucky you'll see some of these agile mountain climbers on the steep canyon walls above you.

Distance: 9.6 miles out and back
Approximate hiking time: 5 hours
Difficulty: Moderate
Trail surface: Dirt and rocks
Best season: Oct through Mar
Water availability: Upper Big Morongo Canyon stream (must be purified)
Other trail users: None
Canine compatibility: Dogs not allowed

Map: USGS Morongo Valley
Fees and permits: None
Trail contact: Big Morongo Canyon Preserve, P.O. Box 780, Morongo Valley, CA 92256; (760) 363-7190; www.bigmorongo.org
Special considerations: During the summer hike early in the day, carry plenty of water, and plan to be finished with the hike by midmorning.

Finding the trailhead: From Palm Springs at the intersection of East Palm Canyon Drive and South Palm Canyon Drive, drive 7.1 miles north on North Palm Canyon Drive, which becomes Indian Canyon Drive, and then turn left onto I-10. Continue west on I-10 for 3.1 miles and then exit onto CA 62. Drive north for 10.9 miles, to the town of Morongo Valley, and turn right on East Drive. Drive 0.2 mile and then turn left on Covington Drive. Drive 0.3 mile to the end of the road at the Big Morongo Canyon Preserve parking area. GPS: N34° 3.034' W116° 34.216'

The Hike

From the trailhead and parking area, walk through the entrance information station and continue a few feet to the start of the Marsh Trail Loop. Turn left and pass both junctions with the Desert Willow Trail by staying right on the Marsh Trail. Next, turn left on the Mesquite Trail and continue to the Big Morongo Canyon Trail, where you'll turn left to start the hike down Big Morongo Canyon.

The canyon immediately narrows as you enter its mouth, but soon widens out a bit where the Canyon Trail joins from the right. Continue down Big Morongo Canyon on the main trail. The small creek is on your left, in dense vegetation. The trail follows an old road, the route of a natural gas pipeline, and is broad and easy to follow.

As the canyon makes a major swing to the east, you'll pass a point where the creek is easily accessible, and then cross it for the first time. After the canyon swings south again, the flowing water comes to an end. From here to the end of the hike, the streambed is a dry, sandy wash.

Shortly after the water ends, you catch the first views of the distant San Jacinto Mountains. There are better views farther downstream. Trail and mileage markers help you find the best route down the broad wash and chart your progress. At the 3.5-mile point, the trail takes a shortcut over a low saddle.

As you near the end of the hike, the view opens out down the canyon, and you soon come to a metal fence spanning the width of the canyon to prevent vehicles from entering the canyon upstream. This is the turnaround point for the hike.

When you return to the upper end of Big Morongo Canyon, you may want to take time to walk a few of the

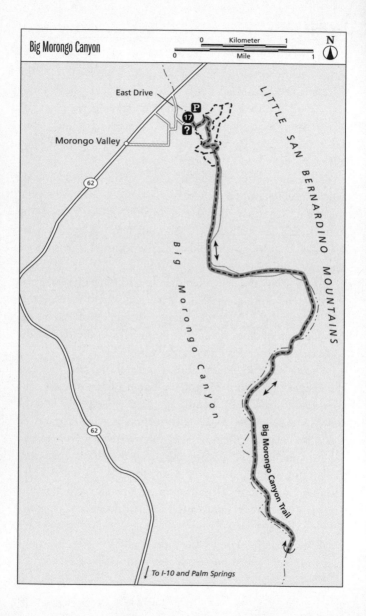

Big Morongo Canyon

0 Kilometer 1
0 Mile 1

N

East Drive

P
17
?

Morongo Valley

62

Big Morongo Canyon

LITTLE SAN BERNARDINO MOUNTAINS

Big Morongo Canyon Trail

62

To I-10 and Palm Springs

short trails and boardwalks that wind through the desert oasis. One of the ten largest cottonwood-willow riparian habitats in California, more than 240 species of birds have been recorded at this internationally recognized site, including several rare species. Other animals that take advantage of this water source are mule deer, raccoons, bobcats, kangaroo rats, gopher snakes, rosy boas, red diamond rattlesnakes, California king snakes, desert spiny lizards, and California tree frogs.

Miles and Directions

0.0 Start at the Big Morongo Canyon Preserve trailhead. Turn left on the Marsh Trail; then stay right on the Marsh Trail at the Desert Willow Trail junction.

0.2 Desert Willow Trail rejoins from the left; stay right on the Marsh Trail.

0.4 Turn left onto the Mesquite Trail.

0.5 Turn left onto the Big Morongo Canyon Trail.

0.8 The Canyon Trail joins from the right; continue straight on the Big Morongo Canyon Trail.

1.6 The trail first crosses the creek as the canyon turns east.

2.1 The flowing creek disappears.

2.2 Enjoy the first view of the distant San Jacinto Mountains.

3.5 The trail takes a shortcut over a low saddle.

4.6 The view opens down the canyon.

4.8 Reach the end of the trail at a steel vehicle barrier fence. Return the way you came.

9.6 Arrive back at the Big Morongo Canyon Preserve trailhead.

Coachella Valley

A section of the Indio Hills is protected in the Coachella Valley Preserve. The San Andreas Fault and several of its branches cut through these hills, creating raw geology in the making at the collision point of the Pacific and North American continental plates. The fault zone has created springs that host several palm oases, including one with a rare desert pool. Easy trails lead past several of these wildlife havens, and also traverse open desert with fine views of the Coachella Valley and the flanking Little San Bernardino and Santa Rosa Mountains.

18 Willis Palms

This loop hike takes you past Willis Palms, a small palm oasis, and then follows a canyon into the Indio Hills. You'll return via a scenic ridge.

Distance: 3.7-mile loop
Approximate hiking time: 2 to 3 hours
Difficulty: Easy
Trail surface: Sand and rocks
Best season: Oct through Mar
Water availability: None
Other trail users: None
Canine compatibility: Dogs not allowed
Map: USGS Myoma
Fees and permits: None

Trail contact: Coachella Valley Preserve, 29200 Thousand Palms Canyon Rd., Thousand Palms, CA 92276; (760) 343-2733 (visitor center); (760) 343-1234 (office); http://coachellavalley preserve.org
Special considerations: During the summer hike early in the day, carry plenty of water, and plan to be finished with the hike by midmorning.

Finding the trailhead: From Palm Springs at the intersection of East Palm Canyon Drive and South Palm Canyon Drive, drive 0.9 mile north on South Palm Canyon Drive (which becomes Indian Canyon Drive), and then turn right on Ramon Road. Continue east 12.6 miles on Ramon Road and then turn left onto Thousand Palms Canyon Road. Drive 0.5 mile and park at the signed Willis Palms Trailhead on the left. GPS: N33° 49.333' W116° 19.433'

The Hike

This easy hike proceeds directly toward Willis Palms, which becomes visible ahead a few yards beyond the trailhead. The main trail passes below the palms—you can take one of several spur trails up into the shady palm oasis.

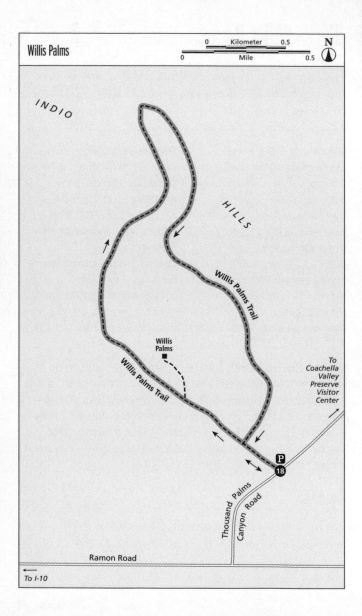

Willis Palms

Kilometer
0   0.5
Mile
0   0.5

N

INDIO

HILLS

Willis Palms Trail

Willis Palms

Willis Palms Trail

To Coachella Valley Preserve Visitor Center

P 18

Thousand Palms Canyon Road

Ramon Road

To I-10

Back on the main trail, continue west to the mouth of a small canyon and follow the trail up the dry wash into this unnamed canyon. Watch for the point where the trail leaves the canyon and climbs out to the right. From here, follow the trail southeast and south along the ridge. After it passes to the north above Willis Palms, the trail drops into a wash and closes the loop. Turn left to return to the trailhead.

During good wildflower seasons, typically March and April after a wet winter, watch for several common flowers along the desert wash and adjoining ridge. These include chia, a spiny, purple flower that favors sandy washes; sand verbena, clusters of small purple flowers that like sandy areas and dunes; rock daisy, a small white daisy; desert sunflower; cream-colored sand-blazing star; and honey mesquite, which has parallel rows of tiny leaves that only appear during wet periods. If it's been wet enough, even creosote bush may bear tiny yellow flowers.

Miles and Directions

0.0 Start at the Willis Palms Trailhead.

0.2 The return trail goes right; stay left, toward the palms.

0.5 Pass a spur trail that climbs right, up into a palm grove; stay left to continue the main loop.

1.0 Follow the trail into the mouth of an unnamed canyon west of the palms.

1.9 The trail leaves the wash and climbs out of the canyon on the right. Follow the trail southeast down the ridge above the wash.

3.6 Reach the end of the loop; turn left to return to the trailhead.

3.7 Arrive back at the Willis Palms Trailhead.

19 Moon Country Loop

This fine loop hike takes you past a palm oasis with a permanent pool and then through a representative portion of the Colorado River Desert in the Indio Hills.

Distance: 4-mile loop
Approximate hiking time: 2 to 3 hours
Difficulty: Easy
Trail surface: Sand and rocks
Best season: Oct through Mar
Water availability: None
Other trail users: None
Canine compatibility: Dogs not allowed
Map: USGS Myoma
Fees and permits: None

Trail contact: Coachella Valley Preserve, 29200 Thousand Palms Canyon Rd., Thousand Palms, CA 92276; (760) 343-2733 (visitor center); (760) 343-1234 (office); http://coachellavalley preserve.org
Special considerations: During the summer hike early in the day, carry plenty of water, and plan to be finished with the hike by midmorning.

Finding the trailhead: From Palm Springs at the intersection of East Palm Canyon Drive and South Palm Canyon Drive, drive 0.9 mile north and then turn right on Ramon Road. Continue east 12.6 miles on Ramon Road and then turn left on Thousand Palms Canyon Road. Drive 2 miles and park at the Coachella Valley Preserve parking area and trailhead, on the left. GPS: N33° 50.283' W116° 18.500

The Hike

From the parking lot, walk west to the signed trailhead for the McCallum Palms Trail and follow this trail west of the visitor center palm grove. The trail follows a shallow ravine for a short distance and passes several private residences.

Follow the signs across the private driveways and stay on the trail. You'll soon pass the first junction with the Moon Country Trail on the left; this is the return trail. Stay right on the McCallum Palms Trail.

As you near the McCallum Palms, turn right on a spur trail which leads about 100 yards north to the palms and a small permanent pond. This pool, a literal oasis in the stark desert, is home to several endangered species, including the desert pupfish. These minnow-like fish are native to desert streams and springs in southeast California, southwest Arizona, and the Colorado River delta in Mexico. Habitat destruction and predation by non-native fish have reduced their natural range to two tributaries of the Salton Sea. Reintroductions have been made throughout their former range, including McCallum Palms.

After returning to the main trail, turn right to continue the loop. The trail passes an area of sand dunes; stay on the trail to avoid disturbing this fragile environment. Sandy areas such as these dunes are home to the sidewinder, a small rattlesnake that has developed a unique method of moving on loose sand. Instead of crawling straight ahead and leveraging off objects as it passes like most snakes, the sidewinder moves sideways by looping its body. This leaves an unmistakable track in the sand. The sidewinder can also burrow rapidly into the sand to escape predators such as hawks.

One predator bird you may be lucky enough to see is the American kestrel. This common falcon is one of the most colorful raptors in the world, with a reddish back and tail and blue-gray wings. Occasionally seen hovering with rapid wing beats while scanning the ground for prey, the American kestrel actually prefers to hunt from perches. Its prey includes lizards, mice, and small birds.

At the four-way junction with the Moon Country Trail near the dunes, turn right to continue the loop counter-clockwise. The Moon Country Trail works its way up onto a low ridge and passes a viewpoint with a great vista of the Indio Hills, nearby McCallum Palms, and the distant grove of palms at the preserve parking area. After the viewpoint, the trail continues along the ridge to the northwest.

Cholla cactus is common along the trail. Cactus adapts to the aridity and heat of the desert by rapidly storing water in the succulent fleshy interior of the stems during wet periods. A tough, waxy skin inhibits loss of moisture by evaporation.

When the Moon Country Trail goes left and drops into the wash, turn left and follow the return trail downstream along the left side of the wash. At the four-way trail junction, stay right. When the loop ends at the junction with the McCallum Palms Trail, stay right to return to the trailhead.

Miles and Directions

0.0 Start at the trailhead at the Coachella Valley Preserve visitor center.

0.5 Pass the Moon Country Trail on the left; stay right toward McCallum Palms.

0.8 Turn right on the spur trail to McCallum Palms.

0.9 Return to the main trail and turn right to continue the loop.

1.2 Reach the four-way junction with the Moon Country Trail; stay right to continue the loop counter-clockwise.

1.4 Reach the viewpoint on the ridgetop.

2.3 The Moon Country Trail goes left and drops into the wash; turn left and follow the left side of the wash downstream.

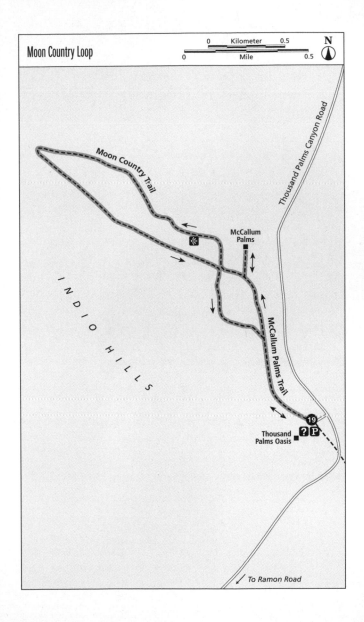

3.2 At the four-way junction with the Moon Country and McCallum Palms Trails, stay right to continue the loop.

3.6 The Moon Country Trail ends; turn right on the McCallum Palms Trail to return to the trailhead.

4.0 Arrive at the trailhead at the Coachella Valley Preserve visitor center.

20 Pushawalla Palms

This loop hike takes you along a scenic ridge in the Indio Hills and past three palm oases.

Distance: 5.2-mile loop
Approximate hiking time: 3 to 4 hours
Difficulty: Moderate
Trail surface: Sand and rocks
Best season: Oct through Mar
Water availability: None
Other trail users: None
Canine compatibility: Dogs not allowed
Map: USGS Myoma
Fees and permits: None

Trail contact: Coachella Valley Preserve, 29200 Thousand Palms Canyon Rd., Thousand Palms, CA 92276; (760) 343-2733 (visitor center); (760) 343-1234 (office); http://coachellavalley preserve.org
Special considerations: During the summer hike early in the day, carry plenty of water, and plan to be finished with the hike by midmorning.

Finding the trailhead: From Palm Springs at the intersection of East Palm Canyon Drive and South Palm Canyon Drive, drive 0.9 mile north and then turn right on Ramon Road. Continue east 12.6 miles on Ramon Road and then turn left on Thousand Palms Canyon Road. Drive 2 miles and park at the Coachella Valley Preserve parking area and trailhead, on the left. GPS: N33° 50.283' W116° 18.500'

The Hike

Start on the east side of the parking area, following the Pushawalla Palms Trail across the desert flat to the east. After crossing Thousand Palms Canyon Road, you'll see the trail ahead where it climbs onto a ridge via a series of steps. At the top of this ridge, the Hidden Palms Trail goes right; this is the return trail. Stay left on the Pushawalla Palms Trail and follow it east along the scenic ridge. Stay on the ridge until the Pushawalla Palms Trail descends left off the ridge.

Stay right at a junction in the desert flat below the ridge and follow the trail down to another junction. Pushawalla Palms is visible a short distance to the northeast; turn left and hike to a point overlooking the palms. Then retrace your steps to the last junction. Turn left to continue the loop on the Hidden Palms Trail.

The route, now following an old road, passes below Horseshoe Palms, several groves found along the south side of the ridge you just hiked. The trail follows the desert plain below the ridge, turning southwest, and then crosses to Hidden Palms. Skirting the palm grove on the right, the Hidden Palms Trail now heads north, back toward the ridge. Stay left at two junctions below the ridge. Once on top of the ridge, the Hidden Palms Trail meets the Pushawalla Palms Trail. Turn left to return to the trailhead.

There is a desert bird that actually prefers to make its home in cactus—the cactus wren. The largest American wren, this wren travels in noisy family groups and is hard to miss when present. Cactus wrens build ball-shaped nests at the tops of cholla cactus or in yucca, using the plant's defenses as its own. These well-adapted birds get most of the water they need from their food, and do not need freestanding water.

Miles and Directions

0.0   Start at the trailhead at the Coachella Valley Preserve visitor center.

0.2   Cross Thousand Palms Canyon Road.

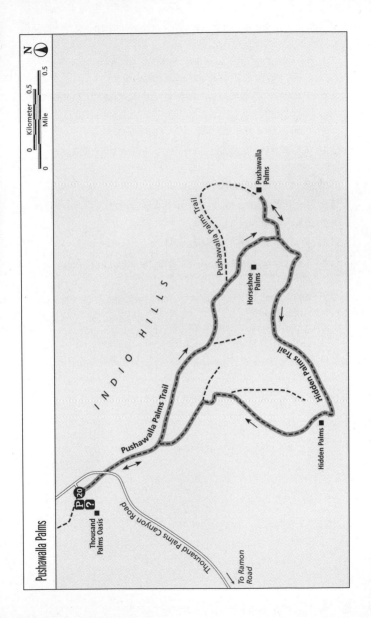

Pushawalla Palms

INDIO HILLS

Pushawalla Palms Trail

Pushawalla Palms Trail

Hidden Palms Trail

Pushawalla Palms

Horseshoe Palms

Hidden Palms

Thousand Palms Oasis

P 20 ?

Thousand Palms Canyon Road

To Ramon Road

N

0   Kilometer   0.5

0   Mile   0.5

0.5 Hidden Palms Trail on the right is the return trail; stay left on the Pushawalla Palms Trail.

1.1 An unnamed trail goes right; stay left and follow the Pushawalla Palms Trail east along the ridgetop.

1.5 Pushawalla Palms Trail descends off the ridge to a junction; stay right.

1.9 Turn left for the side hike to Pushawalla Palms.

2.1 Arrive at Pushawalla Palms. Return to the loop the way you came.

2.3 Turn left to continue the loop on the Hidden Palms Trail.

3.6 The trail passes to the right of Hidden Palms.

4.2 Stay left at a trail junction.

4.4 Stay left at a trail junction.

4.8 Turn left on the Pushawalla Palms Trail to return to the trailhead.

5.2 Arrive back at the trailhead at the Coachella Valley Preserve visitor center.

Clubs and Trail Groups

Coachella Valley Hiking Club: (760) 345-6234; www
.cvhikingclub.net

Desert Trails Hiking Club: PO Box 10401, Palm Desert,
CA 92255; www.deserttrailshiking.com

Sierra Club San Gorgonio Chapter: PO Box 5425,
Riverside, CA 92517; (951) 684-6203; http://sangorgonio
.sierraclub.org

About the Author

The author has a serious problem—he doesn't know what he wants to do when he grows up. Meanwhile, he's done such things as wildland fire fighting, running a mountain shop, flying airplanes, shooting photos, and writing books. He's a backcountry skier, climber, figure skater, mountain biker, amateur radio operator, river runner, and sea kayaker—but the thing that really floats his boat is hiking and backpacking. No matter what else he tries, the author always comes back to hiking—especially long, rough, cross-country trips in places like the Grand Canyon. Some people never learn. But what little he has learned, he's willing to share with you— via his books, of course, but also via his websites, blogs, and whatever works. His website is BruceGrubbs.com.

His other FalconGuides include: *Basic Essentials: Using GPS*; *Best Easy Day Hikes Albuquerque*; *Best Easy Day Hikes Flagstaff*; *Best Easy Day Hikes Las Vegas*; *Best Easy Day Hikes Sedona*; *Best Easy Day Hikes Tucson*; *Best Hikes Near Phoenix*; *Camping Arizona*; *Desert Hiking Tips*; *Explore! Joshua Tree National Park*; *Explore! Mount Shasta Country*; *Grand Canyon National Park Pocket Guide*; *Falcon Guide to Saguaro National Park and the Santa Catalina Mountains*; *Hiking Arizona*; *Hiking Arizona's Superstition and Mazatzal Country*; *Hiking Great Basin National Park*; *Hiking Northern Arizona*; *Hiking Oregon's Central Cascades*; *Joshua Tree National Park Pocket Guide*; *Mountain Biking St. George and Cedar City*; *Mountain Biking Flagstaff and Sedona*; and *Mountain Biking Phoenix*.